Weapons in the theatre

Weapons in the theatre

Arthur Wise

LONGMANS

LONGMANS, GREEN AND CO LTD
London and Harlow
Associated companies, branches and representatives throughout the world

© *Arthur Wise 1968*
First Published 1968

Printed by Spottiswoode, Ballantyne and Co, Ltd, London and Colchester

For Nick

'ever on guard: no weakness in defence'

Contents

Illustrations

All photographs were reproduced by courtesy of Swords of York Ltd.

Acknowledgements

This book is concerned with the use of weapons in the theatre, in film and in television. It is not a book about weapons as such: all the illustrations, for example, are of weapons specially manufactured for the theatre. They are not in any sense *authentic*. Nor does the book contain an accurate survey of the styles of fighting through the centuries. These are considerations for the historian, and I am no historian. It is an attempt to answer two essentially theatrical questions:

1 What is it that makes dramatists, particularly of the Elizabethan period, so preoccupied with scenes of physical violence, and

2 How are the director and the actor to handle such scenes?

I have, of course, read quite widely in the field of weapons and in the field of theatre. I have visited countless collections of arms. I have manufactured weapons and had them tested in performance, to prove my conviction that specially designed weapons are necessary for use in the theatre. In the process I have climbed on the shoulders of a great many people—archeologists, historians, professional fight-arrangers, blacksmiths, saddlers, Shakespearean scholars, museum curators, directors and actors. I am indebted to all of them. Without them, neither theories nor weapons to support the theories could have been produced.

In particular, I should like to thank the following for their help and support during the project out of which this book arises:

Ace Body Builders, Morley; Donald Burton, Royal Shakespeare Company, Stratford upon Avon; City Leather Company, York; Herbert Clarkson, H. Clarkson and Son, York; The Curator, Römisch-Germanisches Zentralmuseum, Mainz; E. J. Dalby, blacksmith, York; Christopher Davy, Leeds Metal Spinning, Leeds; Christopher Denys, Bristol Old Vic Company, Bristol; Dunlop and Ranken Ltd, Leeds; Gareth Lloyd Evans, Institute of Advanced Shakespearean Studies, Stratford upon Avon; Harris Brushworks Ltd, Stoke Prior; George Hauger, The University, Leeds; Minster Engineers, York; Jack Mitchley, County Drama Organizer, Essex; Bryan Mosley, actor, Leeds; John Neville, The Playhouse, Nottingham; Robert Patterson, curator of the Castle Museum, York, and staff; George G. Pemberton, saddler, Long Marston; Warren Sellers, licenced victualler, Mason's Arms, York; K. H. Simpkin, bank manager, Leeds; G. D. Simpson, blacksmith, Wheldrake; Robert Walker, Wadkin Ltd, York; Christopher, Susan and Julia Wise, York, in particular for their work in connection with the manufacture of weapons for the BBC production *Spread of the Eagle*; Jonas Woodhead and Sons Ltd, suspension manufacturers, Leeds; Yorkshire Evening Press, York.

I should like to express my especial gratitude to my colleagues in Swords of York Ltd, Ossie and Ella Heppell of Heppell Shopfitting, York, and Nan Wise, and to my friends Eric Hope of the Castle Museum, York, and Derek Ware, director of HAVOC, London.

We have been unable to trace the copyright owner of *Cyrano De Bergerac* by Edmond Rostand, translated by Gladys Thomas and Mary F. Guillemard and would appreciate any information that would enable us to do so.

Arthur Wise, York 1968

1

The Perennial Complaint

An article appearing in the *Illustrated Sporting and Dramatic News* of 24 April 1886 complains that in a period where such attention is paid to historical accuracy in Shakespearean production, the use of the sword should have been neglected. The *Hamlet* fight 'deserves to be reproduced with accuracy, in order, when taken in conjunction with the passages in the text relating to it, to convey a correct impression of the poet's meaning'. 'I would have each mimic combat shown as he [Shakespeare] must have, in his mind's eye, conceived it.'

Sir Guy Laking, writing in the *Connoisseur* of June 1911, complained of Sir Beerbohm Tree's production of *Henry IV* at the Haymarket Theatre, that Falstaff was 'armed with a weapon which d'Artagnan could have hardly lived to see in fashion, whilst his disreputable companions wore headpieces that had become obsolete before the Battle of Crecy'. Writing of Mansfield's *Richard III* at the Globe in 1889, he says, 'stock suits of quasi-Gothic armour were requisitioned from Birmingham . . . swords from the recesses of the costumier's wardrobe. . . . The effect of this method of arming on Mr Egerton Castle's finely arranged fights was to create an unreality which marred the final scenes . . .'

These complaints are typical of many. Egerton Castle himself says,

Actors also, who, in every other case, are most particular about historical accuracy, generally dispose of all questions relative to fighting by referring them to the first fencing-master at hand; and accordingly one sees Laertes and Hamlet with the utmost sangfroid going through a 'salute' which, besides being perfectly unmanageable with rapiers, was only established in all its details some fifty years ago. There would indeed be less anachronism in uncorking a bottle of champagne to fill the king's beaker than there is in Hamlet correctly lunging, reversing his point, saluting carte and tierce, &c.—foil fencing, in fact—in spite of the anticipation raised by Osric's announcement that the bout should be played with rapier and dagger.

Again in *Romeo and Juliet*:

. . . He tilts

With piercing steel at bold Mercutio's breast;
Who, all as hot, turns deadly point to point,

And, with a martial scorn, with one hand beats
Cold death aside, and with the other sends
It back to Tybalt, whose dexterity
Retorts it.   (Act III, sc. 1.)

It really seems that a single passage like this (and many such occur in the Elizabethan dramatists), might have suggested the probability of a rapier fight being a very different thing indeed from a modern fencing bout, though certainly not less exciting.[1]

The Historical Argument

But clearly these writers are all specialists in the historical study of weapons and the different styles in which they were used. A specialist is notoriously aghast at what seems to him to be the complete ignorance of most of us concerning even the most elementary facts of his specialist study. Such an attitude is understandable but seemingly irrelevant. An actor or director, confronted by the complaints of Sir Guy Laking, for example, would be justified in saying that the theatre is concerned not with historical accuracy for its own sake but with theatrical effectiveness. Indeed, he could reverse the process to prove his point, and complain that although the bloody duel between the Duke of Hamilton and Lord Mohun in November of 1712 was an historical fact, it was theatrically ineffective. Both combatants fell dead, impaled on one another's swords, and that was that. A damp November morning in Hyde Park; no fanfare of trumpets, no dramatic climax, no clamouring audience.

The historian would protest that the duel was fought in deadly earnest. It was not meant to be judged by theatrical standards. The man of the theatre would riposte that similarly a theatrical fight could not be judged in historical terms, but only in terms of its theatrical fitness. The combat in history ends in death. The combat in the theatre must only appear to do so.

Referring to the Hamlet–Laertes fight, Egerton Castle says:

The introduction in the play of rapier and dagger at the Danish Court during the Middle Ages is, of course, no less an anachronism than that of a small sword bout in the performance, but if the actor's part be to carry out the author's ideas, it is certainly a wonder that greater care should never have been bestowed on that scene.

This is to introduce another argument, the argument of theatrical fitness. The theatre man might disagree over the interpretation of the phrase, 'to

[1] *Schools and Masters of Fence.*

2

carry out the author's ideas', but it is likely that he would see it as his function to interpret an author's intentions in as successful theatrical terms as possible.

Theatrical Fitness

It is strange, certainly, that the realist tradition in the theatre, which has laboured so hard at times over the historical accuracy of an eighteenth-century waistcoat button, should have ignored so consistently the historical accuracy of the weapon to be worn alongside such a button. But at bottom this demonstrates an inconsistency, no more. What is profoundly more strange is that the nature of those fights which appear in so many of the 'classical' plays of the English theatre, has hardly ever been related to the total dramatic development. This is a theatrical, not an historical, failure and as such of prime importance.

In considering the argument of historical accuracy we should return to the fundamental question posed by Appia: 'Let us ask what we are looking for in the theatre.' Is there, indeed, to be any relationship between the author's intention and the final performance in the theatre? Are we to treat a dramatist's work merely as the jumping-off place for our own theatrical fancies, a core around which we might form our own associations; or are we faithfully to represent in theatrical terms what we take to be his intention? In either case we will expect to be consistent. Our view of *Hamlet* may be such and such, but in the theatre it must be consistent. Once we have succeeded in the creation of a particular character, everything that char-acter says and does and wears must be consistent. If not, the character will fall apart before the eyes of an audience and the entire theatrical fabric, the logic of unreality, will disintegrate. We shall be left staring across the foot-lights at men and women dressed like buffoons.

'What a man believes may be ascertained,' says Bernard Shaw, 'not from his creed, but from the assumptions on which he habitually acts.'[1] Action, behaviour, may be interpreted widely. It may include his treatment of his wife, his reaction to moral difficulty, his manners when intoxicated. It will embrace his movement and his speech habits. It will certainly include his choice of clothes. One woman will wear a wide-brimmed hat, another would not be seen dead in a hat of any sort. Such choice is essentially an outer reflection of what a person essentially is. Put Macbeth in velvet knickerbockers and he ceases to be Macbeth. It is not in the nature of Macbeth to wear such a garment. Perhaps, then, we are right to expend such labour in the choice of a waistcoat button for Sir Peter Teazle. We would do so because such a detail would add to an audience's impression of

[1] *Man and Superman.*

3

what Sir Peter is as an individual human being. We would do so, that is, out of theatrical rather than historical necessity.

The Arm and the Man

For most of us there are three kinds of weapon. There is that cumbersome piece behind glass in the museum. Only by an enormous stretch of the imagination can we picture how it might be used. There is the theatrical weapon that we have seen wielded so dashingly, and apparently so weight-lessly, on the films. What horrors would have lain in store for all those demure Infantas had it not been for the mayhem created in their protection by the rapier of some celluloid Don Juan? Finally, there is the modern fencing weapon, so light, so fragile, so finely balanced, surrounded by such an aura of esoteric mystery that in action its parries and ripostes are incom-prehensible to a non-fencer. None of them can carry us back successfully to the point that in the theatre we must reach, the point where we can appreciate the relationship between a man and the weapon he carried. A man seen now in the street with a sword in his hand is either the curator of a museum or a modern fencer. Neither has the relationship to the sword he carries that Macbeth must have to his. The curator is going to hang the weapon on a wall. The fencer is going to enjoy an evening in the gymna-sium. But when Macbeth appears, sword in hand, he is going to his death.

Until the late eighteenth century, the sword was for use in personal combat. Domenico Angelo[1] was still concerned in 1763 with teaching a method of defence against a serious attack. Even as late as 1781, John McArthur[2] was primarily concerned with the sword in combat. Until comparatively recently then, more was at stake in a man's choice of a weapon than in his choice of a waistcoat button. We might reasonably conclude that more of what a man essentially was, was reflected in the weapon he carried than in the clothes he wore.

William Bonney—Billy the Kid—described by the late Gary Cooper as 'a homicidal moron from the slums of New York', is reputed to have killed twenty-one men in as many years. We might describe the weapon with which Bonney carried out this slaughter, as a six-shot, single-action, cartridge-loading weapon, with a calibre of ·44 and an effective range varying with the skill of the user. But it is unlikely that this is the way in which Bonney thought of it. His real relationship with the weapon was an extension of himself. It was his hatred, his frustration, his drive to power, made manifest. The bullet was not so much lead, but rather a part of him-self reaching out dominating a situation. The weapon, in fact, was the man.

[1] *Ecole des Armes.*
[2] *Army and Navy Gentleman's Companion.*

4

Bonney was not the man to have carried a no. 3 bore garden gun. It is not in the nature of such a weapon to canalize the power and hatred of a man like Bonney.

The relationship of a man to the weapon he carried is characterized by his view of himself. It is a direct extension of himself. It is his view of how best he can defend himself and how best he can manifest his aggressiveness.

The argument is not any longer the one of historical accuracy for its own sake. It is essentially a theatrical argument. If it is our intention in the theatre to project a consistent and coherent image of a character, then we must choose a weapon that is in keeping with such a character, since that weapon is essentially part of that character.

The Background of the Elizabethan Audience

This 'character argument' is not, of course, the whole story. If we are to represent faithfully the author's intention, we must not only consider that intention in purely theatrical terms, but also in relation to the audience for whom the work was intended. Despite the 'Literary Drama' of the nineteenth century, a play is something to be performed in a theatre before an audience. The audience is part of the total situation and no playwright who knows his business ignores it. We can assume, then, that the Elizabethan audience that watched the *Hamlet* fight saw a good deal more in it than do audiences nowadays. They knew a rapier from a short sword, and they were well aware of the battle being fought throughout the finest period of Elizabethan drama between the exponents of the two weapons.

Henry VIII had encouraged fencing to such an extent that Roger Ascham[1] compares its popularity with the neglect of archery. In 1540 the king granted Letters Patent to the London Masters of Defence. Although for some years previously it had been safe to admit publicly that one ran a school of fence, only in the mid sixteenth century was such an occupation officially recognized. The London Masters had virtually a monopoly of the training of fencers and they taught the traditional English weapons, in particular the sword and buckler. It was against this background that the Italian, Rocco Bonetti, opened a school for the teaching of the newly introduced rapier. The date was about 1576. Shakespeare at the time was about twelve. Bonetti was doubly infuriating to the Masters; he was trespassing on their monopolistic preserve, and he was a foreigner teaching a foreign weapon.

Until that time the systems of fencing taught by the Masters, appear to have been quite unsystematic. What a particular Master regarded as his own favourite move, he tended to invest with universal application. For

[1] *Toxophilus.*

some years before Bonetti's explosive appearance on the London scene, the Italians had been paying logical attention to the use of the sword. They had evolved the rapier as a more suitable weapon for personal combat than the old broadsword and they had developed a coherent system of using it, based on scientific principles. Such principles, of course, were not unknown in England. It had for some time been considered important for a gentleman to visit Italy as part of his education. It was inevitable that as a result he should become acquainted not only with the rapier but with the current theories concerning its use. He would return to England, having heard of Agrippa and Grassi, both of whom insisted on the superiority of the thrust over the cut. Perhaps he would look round for someone who might further his education in the new weapon.

Into such a climate came Bonetti, buying his fencing premises from John Lyly, the playwright. He was followed by Jeronimo, who might well have been his son, and in 1590 Vincentio Saviolo, the Italian Master from Padua, joined Jeronimo in Blackfriars. Together they taught the technique of the rapier and derided the traditional English weapon.

In 1599 George Silver published his *Paradoxes of Defence*. From it we have some idea of the conflict that existed between the two schools of thought. Silver, English gentleman to the core, abuses the rapier and all its exponents. So convinced was he of the superiority of the traditional English weapons that he, together with his brother Toby, issued a challenge to the two Italians to fight in public at the *Belle Sauvage* with an astonishing array of weapons, ranging from single rapier to battle-axe. The Italians, observes Silver with scorn, neglected to appear. Later Jeronimo, equipped with rapier and dagger, was killed by a man called Cheese, armed with the English sword. Silver records the event with unconcealed satisfaction. It is of theatrical interest to note that in plays of the day the conflict between the traditional English weapons and the foreign rapier appears almost as a class symbol.

'Shall I strike it with my partizan?' says Marcellus, staring at the ghost of Hamlet's father. Yet Hamlet and Laertes fight with rapiers.

'Enter Sampson and Gregory with swords and bucklers of the house of Capulet', says the stage direction to the first act of *Romeo and Juliet*. Yet Romeo, Tybalt and Mercutio fight with rapiers.

A Royal Warrant issued by James I in 1605 gave the Masters of Defence the highest status they had ever had—or were ever to have. This granted them the power to control legally the teaching of fencing by unlicensed people. The qualification of *Scholar*, *Free Scholar*, *Provost* or *Master* in the gild of Masters of the Noble Science of Defence was bestowed by 'playing a prize'. The procedure consisted in demonstrating in public one's skill with a wide range of weapons. Although the gild's intentions in these 'prize fights' were serious, such fights were understandably very popular with the London populace, simply as spectacles of masculine prowess. They were accompanied by processions and music and a good deal of showmanship. When it was not possible to get the necessary permission from the City Fathers to conduct such prizes, the exhibition took place outside the City limits.

Holinshed[1] says that almost everyone over eighteen or twenty carried at least a dagger at his back or his side. All nobility carried swords or rapiers as well, and so did all such a man's servants. No one travelled without a sword, except a minister, and he carried a dagger. According to Stow,[2] every haberdasher sold bucklers.

This was the scene against which the Elizabethan dramatists wrote. We may conclude that they, along with every other Londoner, had a wide general knowledge of weapons and the controversies concerning their use which raged at the time.

Fighters and Actors

But this is perhaps not sufficient to account for the number of fights and references to weapons that appear in plays of the period. Football is popular as a spectacle at the moment, so is wrestling, but we find hardly a contemporary play being produced with a single reference to either, let alone whole scenes necessary to the dramatic action being played in a football stadium or a wrestling ring.

There was, it seems, a particular relationship in the later sixteenth century between fencers and players which made actors and writers even more conversant with the activities of the fencing fraternity than was the general populace. This particular relationship is shown in many ways. The City Fathers of London, had as low a regard for the theatre as for the Masters of Defence. Both had the greatest difficulty in obtaining the Fathers' permission for public performances within the City. Both were compelled to operate mostly outside the City limits in Blackfriars and elsewhere. 'After the dissolution of the monasteries, the fencers, together with their fellow outcasts from the City Paradise, the stage-players and the dancers, had congregated in the Blackfriars', says Aylward.

The Fight as Entertainment

The players were declared entertainers. On the face of it, the Masters playing a prize had a different aim, but from the spectators' point of view such

[1] *Chronicles.*
[2] *Annals.*

a prize must have been regarded largely as a spectacle, an entertainment. Any competent dramatist must have been aware of the entertainment value of the well-conducted fight and we must admit this as being at least one of the reasons for the existence of so many displays of arms, in the Elizabethan theatre. It is frequently argued that the martial plays of Shakespeare are in a sense propaganda for a regime threatened at one time by foreign invasion and at another pushing its power out into the farthest corners of the earth. But any man of the theatre knows the real reason for a dramatist to put a scene in a play; it is simply because it is dramatically effective, because in the broadest sense it has an entertainment contribution to make. Then again, players and fencers frequently used the same venues: 'There were certain attractive venues just outside the limits of their [the City Fathers'] jurisdiction, such as the Artillery Garden in Bishopsgate Without, the Theatre and the Curtain in Holywell, near Shoreditch.'[1]

We can assume that at least a proportion of the spectators at a prize played one day at the *Curtain* or the *Theatre*, would be members of the audience at the play produced there on the next. G. B. Harrison says, 'The tragedy of *Romeo and Juliet* was first produced in 1595, and was thus one of the plays which the Lord Chamberlain's Company performed during their occupation of the *Theatre* in Shoreditch'.[2] And *Romeo and Juliet*, it must be admitted, contains some of the most spectacular fighting scenes of any Elizabethan play. Such audiences would make the highest demands regarding the execution of the theatrical fights, since they would have specialist experience of combat between the most skilled exponents in the country. Indeed, de Witt's drawing of the *Swan*,[3] shows a place very suitable for the playing of a prize. We are accustomed to think of a fighting ring as something enclosed by ropes, but Silver, in his challenge to Jeronimo and Saviolo, mentions something much more like the raised stage shown by de Witt in 1595, 'where he that went in his fight faster backe then he ought, of Englishman or Italian, shold be in danger to breake his necke off the Scaffold'.

Actors as Fighters

Would mere players be able, in *Romeo and Juliet* for example, to produce swordsmanship to satisfy such an audience? We can only conclude that such must have been the case. No dramatist would have entered into open competition with the prize fights, unless he was sure that his contribution had a reasonable chance of being compared favourably with them. Sup-

[1] *The English Master of Arms.*
[2] *Romeo and Juliet:* introduction to Penguin edition.
[3] *British Drama.*

porting this is the fact that Richard Tarlton, the great comic actor, was himself a Master of Defence and therefore one of the outstanding fencers of London.[1] It seems likely that the spectators at his Master's prize, which he was 'allowed' on 23 October 1587, would also be part of the audiences for his play performances.

Ben Jonson gives, in *Cynthia's Revels*,[2] a parody of a Bill of Challenge such as was issued by a prizor's Master. Ben Jonson, indeed, gives many references to fencing in his plays that indicate a high degree of specialist knowledge. To an audience of today, whole passages must be quite incomprehensible. Fly, in *The New Inne*,[3] says—

> Go by, Hieronymo.

Tipto: What was he?

Fly: The Italian
> That play'd with abbot Antony i' the Fryers,
> And Blinkin-sops the bold.

Tip: I marry, those
> Had fencing names, what's become o' them?

Host: They had their times, and we can say, they were.
> So had Caranza his: so had Don Lewis.

Tip: Don Lewis of Madrid is the sole master
> Now of the world.

'Carranza and Don Luis Pacheco were household names in England about the end of the sixteenth century, if their frequent occurrence in the works of the dramatists of that period is any criterion', says Castle. And if we delve we can discover that Anthony ffenreuther and John Blinkinsopps were both 'allowed Master' in 1583, a fact no doubt known to a contemporary audience in the same way that we might know the names of Henry Cooper and Mohamed Ali, or as an earlier generation knew who was being referred to when they sang the line, 'to meet Jack Johnson as the great white hope'. It is doubtful whether any part of this entire scene from *The New Inne* means anything at all nowadays to an audience without considerable specialist knowledge of Elizabethan fighting.

We should remember, too, that Ben Jonson wrote of the Masters and the fights not merely as an interested observer. On 22 September 1598 he killed a fellow-actor, Gabriel Spencer, in a duel at Hoxton. He was found guilty of manslaughter, spent time in prison, had his goods confiscated and his

---

[1] *Schools and Masters of Fence:* 'These details are found in MS. No. 2530. XXVI. D. Sloanian Collection, Brit. Mus.'
[2] *Act V, sc. iii.*
[3] *Act II, sc. v.*

left thumb branded. Middleton, Dekker and Marston all refer to weapons and fights in a way suggesting a close knowledge of them. Against this background, then, Hamlet first met Laertes, Viola and Aguecheek went through their comic performance with rapiers and Macbeth first went to his death.

We can assume that a dramatist putting so many fighting scenes into his works would be certain that his performers would acquit themselves effectively before an audience that was accustomed to seeing the prize fights of the Masters of Defence and that knew and appreciated the moves made.

2

The Sheer Mechanics

We no longer have audiences equipped with specialist knowledge of old swordplay. What are we to do with these troublesome fight scenes in contemporary productions? Can they be cut altogether? Certainly we could justify such action, for the audience for which the plays were written has passed.

Hamlet is worth investigating from this point of view. Is it possible to rid ourselves of the fight simply by cutting? The very least we must take out from Act V, sc. ii, is from the instruction, 'They play' to Hamlet's, 'Nay, come again.' A matter of thirty-four lines. But this will scarcely do, for the scene now reads:

King:
> Set me the stoups of wine upon that table.
> If Hamlet give the first or second hit,
> Or quit in answer of the third exchange,
> Let all the battlements their ordnance fire;
> The king shall drink to Hamlet's better breath;
> And in the cup an union shall he throw,
> Richer than that which four successive kings
> In Denmark's crown have worn. Give me the cups;
> And let the kettle to the trumpet speak,
> The trumpet to the cannoneer without,
> The cannons to the heavens, the heavens to earth,
> 'Now the king drinks to Hamlet!' Come, begin;
> And you, the judges, bear a wary eye.

Hamlet: Come on, sir.

From which point we cut to—

> [*The Queen falls.*]

Osric: Look to the queen there, ho!

Horatio: They bleed on both sides. How is it, my Lord?

Osric: How is it, Laertes?

Laertes: Why, as a woodcock to mine own springe, Osric;
> I am justly kill'd with mine own treachery . . .

And so on. There it is when we have cut the actual physical fight, the actual play of weapons. And, of course, it simply does not make sense, either as an argument or dramatically. The surgery has been too localized; we must cut more generally.

We must cut the preceding speech of the king. We must cut the king's reference to 'the foils'. We must cut the reference to 'the wager'. We must cut, in fact, the entire scene, the entire end of the play as it now stands.

Another question arises: what do we mean by a fight? Do we mean the physical clash of weapons in full view of the audience between two or more opponents, or do we mean any violent use of weapons? And if the latter—and where precisely do we draw the line?—then what are we to do with Hamlet's slaying of old Polonius? And if we cut that, how are we to get rid of Polonius? If he dies by natural causes during Laertes' absence, does Ophelia go mad? Can Laertes himself, no longer filled with hatred against the man who has stabbed to death his father, be persuaded to use a poisoned weapon against Hamlet?—but then, the question is now merely of academic interest since we have already cut the fight.

We could pursue the policy further, only to find that we have destroyed the entire structure of the play. In order to resurrect it we should have to rewrite it. In particular, we should have to rewrite the whole of the final scene at the very least, and if we are to rewrite so completely, have we any longer a play by Shakespeare? Is it not now some other play by someone else? We are forced to conclude that, at least as regards *Hamlet* by William Shakespeare, the fight between Hamlet and Laertes is woven so deeply into the whole structure that it cannot be cut without changing the play fundamentally.

Hamlet, of course, may not be the best choice for our purpose. We should try our knife on *Macbeth*. We face the same problems here. We cut the end, the actual fights between Macbeth and Young Siward and Macbeth and Macduff, only to find strands from earlier scenes that must be excised—

Macduff: . . . front to front
    Bring thou this fiend of Scotland and myself;
    Within my sword's length set him; if he 'scape,
    Heaven forgive him too![1]

Again we must rewrite, at the very least, the final scenes and excise strands relevant to them throughout the play.

We find the same with *Romeo and Juliet*. We must cut the whole introductory scene and rewrite it. We must cut and rewrite most of the first scene of Act III—and yet, if Romeo doesn't kill Tybalt, how can he be banished? And if he is not banished, we must rewrite much of the later scenes of the play. Again, if we cut the fight scenes on the grounds that they

[1] *Act IV, sc. iii.*

are theatrically difficult to handle and frequently not geared to contemporary audiences, we find we are left with a piece so rewritten that it can no longer be ascribed to Shakespeare.

The Fight and the Dramatic Structure

We have assumed that a writer, particularly of theatrical pieces, writes in a way determined by his times. In a time when the sword was an article of constant wear and when its use was frequently discussed and demonstrated, it is reasonable that such facts should be embodied in writing of the period. It is reasonable, too, that in such a period a writer of plays should make some attempt to capitalize for his own purposes the entertainment value of the prize fights organized by the Masters of Defence. Since the sword means little to us nowadays and few of us have ever heard of the Masters of Defence, we have attempted to handle the fight scenes by simply cutting them. As a result we have seen that they are enmeshed a good deal more deeply in the total dramatic structure than at first sight appeared.

It becomes apparent that we cannot regard the fights as something in isolation, something injected arbitrarily into an already coherent structure simply to pander to the caprices of a contemporary audience. We are compelled to see them as an integral part of the whole dramatic structure, revealing character, furthering action, in such a way that they cannot be lifted out of the total fabric without irrevocably destroying it.

Let us clear away first those references in the plays of Shakespeare, for example, relating to fights and weapons that have today frankly a good deal less significance for us than they must have had for contemporary audiences. Mercutio, for example, dying after his encounter with Tybalt, says— '. . . a braggart, a rogue, a villain, that fights by the book of arithmetic'. Earlier, describing Tybalt, he has said—

> More than Prince of Cats. O he's the courageous captain of compliments: he fights as you sing prick-song, keeps time, distance and proportion, he rests, his minim rests, one, two and the third in your bosom: the very butcher of a silk button, a duellist, a duellist, a gentleman of the very first house of the first and second cause, ah the immortal passado, the punto reverso, the hay.
>
> *Benvolio:* The what?
>
> *Mercutio:* The pox of such antic lisping affecting fantasies, these new tuners of accents: by Jesu, a very good blade, a very tall man; a very good whore. Why is not this a lamentable thing grandsire, that we should be thus afflicted with these strange flies: these fashion-mongers, these

13

pardon-mes, who stand so much on the new form, that they cannot sit
at ease on the old bench. O their bons, their bons.

As an audience, do we now need to know that it was Jeronimo de Carranza,
the Spaniard, who outlined a system of fighting that appears very much to
be based on 'the book of arithmetic'?[1] Do we need to know that, according
to Castle, 'Carranza's is the first of a long series of ponderous Spanish
treatises on the "raison demonstrative", in which the ruling principle, after
the Aristotelian method, is the "conocimiento de la cosa por su causa", and
the purpose, to demonstrate that a perfect theoretical knowledge must
infallibly lead to victory, notwithstanding grievous physical disadvantage',
in order to appreciate Mercutio's, 'a gentleman of the very first house of the
first and second cause'? Do we need to know that Mercutio's speech
beginning, 'The pox of such antic lisping affecting fantasies . . .' seems
to prelude George Silver's sweeping attack on the introduction of the rapier
by Spanish and Italian Masters of Defence, and that 'the very butcher of a
silk button' appears to be a reference to a story quoted later by Silver:
'Signor Rocco, thou that art thought to be the onely cunning man in the
world with thy weapon, thou that takest upon thee to hit anie Englishman
with a thrust upon anie button. . . .'?

Probably we need none of this rather specialist knowledge as an audience.
These are passing references that have died and we do not feel the loss.
In some cases they may be cut; in others we may gloss over them as one
may gloss over references in a conversation to persons one doesn't know,
and still get the meat of what is being said. For the most part, they are not
references deeply embedded in plot or character or dramatic development.
The question of whether the actor can be as ignorant of their meaning, is of
course another matter.

But this does not throw light on the problem of the Hamlet–Laertes
fight, for example, or upon the Macbeth–Macduff fight, nor for that
matter upon the Romeo–Tybalt fight. These are all bedded in plot, and
character is revealed through them. They are all, in fact, essential elements
of the dramatic action and we must look at them for a moment in this light.

Too much has already been said about *Hamlet*, the play and the character, to warrant further critical comment. It is sufficient to remind ourselves
that Hamlet is given throughout most of the play to a great deal of talk
about action without in fact acting. He is a man under increasing pressure
from within and without. He is constantly being urged by the ghost of his
father to do something to right the wrong. He is a man being wound up
like a spring from the very opening of the play. He grows more and more
explosive, without in fact exploding. Even at the moment when he takes up

---

[1] *Libro de Jeronimo de Carranza, que trata de la filosofia de las armas y de su destreza, y de la
agresion y defension Christiana.*

his 'foil' and faces Laertes, there is no indication that the bomb that has been charged and primed so carefully throughout four and a half acts will go off. What is it, what small occurrence, that finally precipitates the explosion that has been impending since the first curtain and results, in a few moments, in the mayhem of those last five minutes of the play?

Hamlet: Come, for the third, Laertes. You but dally;
    I pray you, pass with your best violence.
    I am afeard you make a wanton of me.
Laertes: Say you so? come on. [*They play*].
Osric: Nothing, neither way.

This is all very controlled, it seems; very civilized. It would not sound amiss in a modern gymnasium as an exchange between two fencers. Then suddenly—

Laertes: Have at you now.
    [*Laertes wounds Hamlet; then, in scuffling, they change rapiers, and Hamlet wounds Laertes.*]
King: Part them! They are incens'd.

The whole scene has changed. No longer are we watching a friendly test of skill. We see now two men, 'incens'd' and mortally wounded. Nor does it end there; once the power of action is released in Hamlet he turns and stabs the king to death. It is interesting to see that both Laertes and the king predecease Hamlet, yet all are stabbed with the same weapon, a weapon unbated and poisoned. Hamlet, we must conclude, is poisoned; the wound delivered by Laertes is only superficial. Yet Hamlet himself strikes with sufficient force and savagery to kill with steel, not poison. It is true that the king himself thinks he is no more than wounded and Hamlet might even succeed in forcing past his uncle's lips the remains of the poison that has killed his mother, but the king's death is too sudden for poison. We can account for it only in terms of a deep and mortal stab wound, a wound caused by the release of all Hamlet's pent-up suffering.

How did this sudden change take place? What was it that suddenly precipitated the whole conflict in action? It was the wound inflicted by Laertes, not a mortal wound but one of treachery sufficient to trigger off the whole sequence of following events. It is the only physical action taken against Hamlet in the entire play; somehow one feels it is the excuse he has been waiting for that will justify for him the unleashing of the terrible force that has been destroying him.

Looking back from the end of the play, we see that the whole outcome has been predestined. We have been prepared throughout for a sudden and violent end. The ghost of Hamlet's father appears in 'warlike form'

15

at the outset. He appears in the guise of physical action. Horatio says of him—

> Such was the very armour he had on
> When he the ambitious Norway combated;
> So frowned he once, when, in an angry parle,
> He smote the sledded Polacks on the ice.

And a moment later—

> But in the gross and scope of my opinion,
> This bodes some strange eruption to our state.

Strange eruption indeed! Hamlet himself is disturbed and prophetic when told of the apparition—

> My father's spirit in arms! all is not well;
> I doubt some foul play: would the night were come!
> Till then sit still, my soul: foul deeds will rise,
> Though all the earth o'erwhelms them, to men's eyes.

Hamlet seems almost to come to action, to resolve the conflict in blood, when he kills Polonius thinking him to be the king. But it is abortive action that comes to nothing. Dramatically, however, it prepares us further for what is inevitably to come. It reveals that action is by now only a little way below the surface. The tension rises further.

Anxious to make the point, we think we see symbolism throughout the play, all auguring the final mayhem, as when Hamlet says to the first player—

> I heard thee speak me a speech once, but it was never acted . . . One speech in it I chiefly loved: 'twas Aeneas' tale to Dido: and thereabout of it especially, where he speaks of Priam's slaughter.

But this is to press the matter too far. It is sufficient to have established that not only is the final fight technically too bound up with the play to be cut, but that it is an essential and integral part of the total dramatic action. No fight, no *Hamlet*.

Briefly, we find the same thing in *Macbeth*. Macbeth has lived by the sword—the sword wins him Cawdor and the crown—can he decently die in bed? After his murder of Duncan and his two chamberlains, of Banquo, of Macduff's wife and family and servants, what end is dramatically possible but Macbeth's violent death by the sword?

In *Romeo and Juliet*, shot through as it is with Renaissance passion and violence, the fights are an integral part of the dramatic fabric. They contribute to the action, plot is dependent upon them, they reflect and reveal character.

16

We find the same in *Othello*. The tension is such that it can only burst from time to time into violence. This violence furthers the plot and is revealing of character. Othello says—

> Dost thou hear, Iago,
> I will be found most cunning in my patience:
> But (dost thou hear) most bloody.

Iago: That's not amiss . . .

And in the same scene—

Othello: How shall I murther him, Iago?

A little later—

Othello: I will chop her into messes: cuckold me!

Earlier in the play he has cried—

> Oh blood, blood, blood.

It is interesting, and significant too, to note that Othello takes pains to select the right weapon for what must be to him the just execution of his wife—

> . . . Yet I'll not shed her blood,
> Nor scar that whiter skin of hers, than snow,
> And smooth as monumental alabaster:
> Yet she must die . . .

And at last he selects his own hands as the execution weapons. There is here a deliberate choice of the most fitting weapon for the task:

Othello: Get me some poison, Iago, this night. I'll not expostulate with her: lest her body and beauty unprovide my mind again: this night Iago.

Iago: Do it not with poison, strangle her in her bed, even the bed she hath contaminated.

Othello: Good, good:
The justice of it pleases: very good.

We have established that if the fights were not more than irrelevancies to the main purpose of the plays, they are technically too deeply enmeshed in them to be cut. We have seen that even if it were possible to cut them, we can no longer do so, since they are an integral part of the dramatic action, furthering plot, revealing character, carrying the action a stage further, adding to or releasing dramatic tension.

17

The Fight and the Weapons

We might see a contemporary political significance in *Julius Caesar* and decide, therefore, to set it in the Germany of Adolf Hitler. We can play *Hamlet* in modern dress, for whatever purpose. We might even set *Macbeth* in the Chicago of the 1920s and establish some measure of theatrical success—up to a point. But again we are bedevilled by the fights. The point is this: is there a relationship between the weapons used and the fight, between the weapons and the characters involved in the fight? Can we use any weapon, provided it is a weapon, or are there restrictions within the play that demand a particular weapon?

It is true that we might regard Hamlet's command, 'Give us the foils', as a stumbling block. The point need not be taken as too important. It is just conceivable that he might say, 'Give us the Smith and Wessons'. There is nothing in specific words in the text that need deter us from using weapons other than foils. If we remember those productions where the word 'foil' has been so misunderstood as to produce from the wardrobe modern fencing foils instead of bated rapiers, we shall see a more fundamental problem. Laertes must wound Hamlet sufficiently to introduce the poison into his system. With a foil of the modern variety this is possible. But in return Hamlet must stab Laertes sufficiently deeply to cause death in a few moments; he must then turn and dispatch the king in the same way. It is stretching the imagination of both audience and actor too far to expect them to believe that this can be done. It is not in the nature of that featherweight practice weapon, the modern fencing foil, to inflict two such wounds. An audience—and an actor—must be shown a weapon which, within the theatrical terms of reference, can be believed capable of performing what it is supposed to perform. The modern foil is unsatisfactory for another reason too. A foil fight between two unskilled modern fencers is not only exceedingly dangerous, but exceedingly maladroit. A foil fight between two skilled modern fencers is so fast, the movements so small, that to an uninitiated audience, it lacks any theatrical interest whatever.

Let us dress Hamlet in presentday costume; let us give him the contemporary weapon, rifle and bayonet. The first objection does not apply here. It is perfectly clear to everyone that a bayonet is capable in itself of stabbing Laertes and the king to death. It will perform that which it is supposed to perform. But we can imagine the final scene—blunted bayonets stuck on the end of rifles, stout masks completely covering the faces and necks of the actors, bodies padded from top to bottom. No doubt we shall decide that such a spectacle is quite out of keeping with the feel of the play. We shall decide, too, that it is theatrically impossible to have the central figures invisible and wellnigh inaudible at such a vital juncture. We shall be left too with the ludicrous spectacle of Hamlet, padded like an elephant, being carried off before Fortinbras to the clatter of trumpets, and the vision of the very burly flights of angels necessary to 'sing thee to thy rest'.

There is a further objection to the rifle and bayonet. We have seen Hamlet throughout four acts, an intelligent, sensitive, anguished being. We have a grasp of the nature of his character. Hamlet is not a cosh boy with a bicycle chain coiled in his pocket, nor is he the sort of person whom we can believe skilled in the use of such a cumbersome weapon as the rifle and bayonet. 'Since he [Laertes] went to France,' says Hamlet, 'I have been in continual practice.' It is unbelievable that it is with the rifle and bayonet that he has been in continual practice. A weapon is an extension of its wielder; the weapon Hamlet uses must be in keeping with Hamlet himself.

There is no way of knowing the nature of the weapons used in the original productions of Shakespeare's plays, but we may guess from internal evidence and from evidence of fighting outside the theatre that they were weapons of the period with their points and edges blunted—bated weapons, foiled weapons.[1] It was these weapons that the writer had in mind when he decided to introduce scenes of physical combat. Certainly, we should solve many of our problems if we were to use genuine Elizabethan rapiers—they are in keeping with the style of the play, they are in keeping with the character.

But we should in some cases finish with a stage floor covered in genuine blood and have the task of looking round for new principals. But there are other disadvantages in authentic weapons than their lethal quality. They are very expensive, they are too heavy now for the speed of modern productions, they are usually in a condition of advanced corrosion. We can add, too, that there is no longer the skill in using weapons amongst most modern actors that we have seen must have been the case with the Elizabethans. But the fundamental argument against authentic weapons is again one of reality: the purpose of an authentic weapon is to kill, the purpose of a theatrical weapon is to *appear* to do so. We must look, then, for other weapons.

The principles governing our choice of weapons for the theatre should be these:

1 A weapon should be as safe as possible. It should appear to be lethal without in fact being so.

[1] Dover Wilson in his introduction to the Shakespeare Association's facsimile of the *Paradoxes of Defence*, says, 'I can see nothing in Shakespeare to show that he knew of buttons.' Although Aylward, *The English Master of Arms*, states that buttons in fact were known at the time, and as an undoubted specialist we must take his word for it, Dover Wilson's general conclusions on this point are clearly correct. A buttoned weapon could not have been faked to poison Hamlet and later stab Laertes and the king to death.

2 The actor and his audience should have no difficulty in believing it capable of performing the task demanded of it.

3 It should not offend against the style of the play.

4 It should be in keeping with the character using it.

5 It should have those main features of a particular period that give it the appearance of historical accuracy.

Style in Fighting

All weapons have certain possibilities and certain clear limitations. A man cannot be killed with certainty at half a mile by a revolver. It is one of the limitations of that weapon that its accuracy cannot be guaranteed over such a distance. By style in fighting, is meant the most successful method of using a weapon, capitalizing to the full its possibilities but at the same time acknowledging its limitations.

There is something to a specialist historian of the use of weapons, that is offensive in the use in *Hamlet* of the modern counter-parry of sixte. Such a person is equally offended by the use of the lunge in Macbeth. Neither movement was invented at the time the plays of the Elizabethan dramatists are set, nor indeed at the time the plays were written. We must consider again for a moment the validity of the purely historical argument in the theatre and again conclude that that which offends historical accuracy is irrelevant, unless at the same time it offends the canons of theatrical art.

We must not make the mistake either, of believing that neither the counter-parry of sixte nor the lunge had been invented at the time Shakespeare was writing, because of a lack of adequate study on the part of the Masters of Fence. A glance at the works of Marozzo, Agrippa, Grassi, Saviolo, George Silver, is sufficient to show that a great deal of thought and experiment was devoted to sword play. If the counter-parry and the lunge had been valuable possibilities with the weapons of the period, it is inconceivable that they would not have been invented. We are forced to the conclusion that only with the introduction of the much lighter weapons of a later period, depending as they did almost exclusively on the use of the point, were such movements possible. Style, then, is related directly to a particular weapon. What is a valid and valuable movement with one weapon, is impossible or useless with another.

But we are not going to use an authentic Elizabethan rapier in *Hamlet*, we are going to use a lighter weapon which has merely the appearance of the real thing. With such a theatrical weapon, movements are possible which would not be possible with the real weapon. Are we then to use a style more in keeping with the weapon we are actually using, or a style in

keeping with the weapon that our theatrical counterpart is supposed to
represent? The counter of sixte is possible and useful with a theatrical
rapier; it is not possible with an Elizabethan rapier. What is to be our
attitude here?

'Let us ask what we are looking for in the theatre.' Are we giving a
display of fighting best suited to a theatrical weapon, without consideration
of dramatic development or character revelation, or are we using a weapon
in a scene which is essentially part of the play, essentially related to character and dramatic action? There can be no valid theatrical argument which
allows us to give a display of fighting skill, quite out of the context of the
play. We are not concerned with a weapon as a weapon, but with the
character using it and the dramatic significance of the circumstances in
which it is being used. The style we are concerned with, then, is not that
best fitted to the theatrical weapon we are using, but that best fitted to the
feeling of the play and to the characters within that play. In *Hamlet* we are
to use a style in keeping with Hamlet, and not in keeping with the theatrical
weapons we are using.

What is that style to be? What is the style of fighting in keeping with,
for instance, the Tybalt–Mercutio fight? There are in this case certain
firm descriptions in the text that make it abundantly clear that the style
is that of Elizabethan rapier play. Benvolio, reporting the fight to the
Prince, says—

> Romeo . . . bid him bethink
> How nice the quarrel was, and urg'd withal
> Your high displeasure: all this uttered,
> With gentle breath, calm look, knees humbly bow'd
> Could not take truce with the unruly spleen
> Of Tybalt deaf to peace, but that he tilts
> With piercing steel at bold Mercutio's breast,
> Who all as hot, turns deadly point to point,
> And with a martial scorn, with one hand beats
> Cold death aside, and with the other sends
> It back to Tybalt, whose dexterity
> Retorts it: Romeo he cries aloud,
> Hold friends, friends part, and swifter than his tongue,
> His agile arm beats down their fatal points,
> And 'twixt them rushes, underneath whose arm,
> An envious thrust from Tybalt, hit the life
> Of stout Mercutio, and then Tybalt fled,
> But by and by comes back to Romeo,
> Who had but newly entertain'd revenge,
> And to't they go like lightning . . .

21

A glance at the reproductions in Castle's *Schools and Masters of Fence* of Fabris's illustrations to his book, *De lo Schermo*, is sufficient to give an idea of the sort of fighting that Benvolio is describing. *De lo Schermo* was published in Copenhagen in 1606. It is of interest, though perhaps not of any great significance, to note that Fabris was at the court of Denmark at the time when Shakespeare was writing *Hamlet*.

The style, then, of a fight in a play is to be that which is in keeping with the play. There are two other reasons why the moves of modern fencing are unsatisfactory. In the first place, a man faced by an opponent whose aim is to kill him, is unlikely to resort to subtle moves which, if they prove slightly ill-timed, will expose him to a fatal thrust. To an audience, a series of subtle finger parries, lunges, parries on the lunge and ripostes, indicates rightly that the fighters are not in earnest: men determined to kill one another and at the same time avoid death themselves, do not behave in that way. In the second place, as we have seen, the moves of modern fencing, when properly executed by accomplished fencers, are invisible to an audience seated more than a few yards away. They are not movements with any theatrical significance.

3

The Possibilities of Violence

The ways in which one man might inflict physical damage on another seem, on the face of it, limitless. In fact this is not the case. The theatrical fight is concerned in essence with two men facing one another, armed with personal weapons. One obvious limitation of the theatrical fight, then, is that the opponents must come within physical striking distance of one another.

There are other limitations, arising from the nature of the human body. A thrust through the chest will probably be fatal, whereas a thrust through the hand will not be. Limitations arise as well from the nature of the weapon itself. A full-blooded cut with the blade of a two-handed axe would undoubtedly be fatal, but a thrust with the same weapon might result in no more than severe bruising. The axe has no point with which a thrust can be made. It is one of its limitations. There are, too, limitations arising from a combination of the nature of the human body and the nature of the weapon being used to attack it. A sword thrust *through* the back is likely to be much more damaging than a sword cut *across* it. Conversely, a sword cut down on the shoulder might do considerably more damage than a thrust through it. It is a question of understanding the limitations and possibilities of both the weapon that is being used and the target that is being attacked.

The Target

Let us look first at the target. For the sake of convenient reference, it can be divided into five main areas of attack, with the subsidiary areas of arms and legs. The diagram on page 24 identifies these areas. If we make an attack in which we intend to hit the target in the right side of the chest with either the cutting edge of the sword or with the point, we can describe this briefly as CUT (or THRUST) C.

Faced with an attack, our opponent is likely to defend himself. He might do this by *parrying* with either his sword or his dagger; that is, by using either sword or dagger to deflect our blade away from his body. In the case of an attack, CUT C, the most likely parry would be one with the sword that carried the attacking blade through the C sector and off the target. Such a defensive move can be described briefly as PARRY C. In rare circumstances, it might be necessary to specify whether the sword or the dagger was used in making the parry.

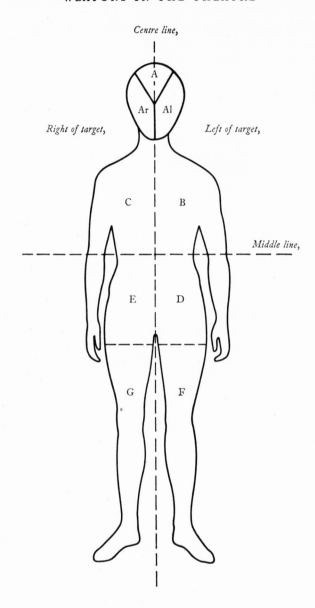

General Movements

Any fight contains two distinct types of movement. There are the specific movements of the individual fighters—the cuts, thrusts and parries—and at the same time there is the general movement of both fighters over the floor. In an authentic fight, this *floor-pattern* is necessarily haphazard, governed as it is by such factors as the weakening of one of the fighters and the existence of natural hazards—trees, chairs, rough ground—which have to be avoided. The floor-pattern in the theatrical fight, however, is very important. The plotting of such a floor-pattern will be considered in detail in chapter 4.

The general movement of a fight is not confined to the floor-pattern. One fighter may jump down from a table, or battle his way up a staircase. This variation in the *pattern of levels* adds a third dimension to the fight. Changes in levels can be suggested in film and television by changes in camera position. In the theatre, however, they must be plotted as part of the actors' total movements.

Since movement exists not only in space but also in time, variations in the rhythm of the fight patterns can be seen as part of the general movement.

This rhythm is of considerable importance in building and releasing the tension of a fight.

Specific Movements

Within this pattern of general movement, the fighters make the specific movements of attack and defence. Every weapon dictates to some extent the specific movements that are possible and useful with it. It is not necessary to consider these movements in relation to every weapon likely to be

used in the theatre. The illustration on page 25, taken from George Silver's *Paradoxes of Defence*, shows a man armed with the English short sword and dagger of the late Elizabethan period. These weapons embrace almost all of the movements that are possible with any other weapon or combination of weapons. Movements possible with the mace or axe are all possible with the short sword. Movements possible with the buckler or cloak, are almost all possible with the dagger. The short sword is capable of thrusting as well as cutting. It can be used for certain defensive moves as well as for attack. If we consider in some detail the movements possible with the short sword and dagger, we shall have covered almost all the movements possible with any other combination of weapons.

The Guards

A guard can be defined as a position from which an attacking or defensive movement might be launched. It is the position taken up at the beginning of any fight. It is the position adopted by a fighter when he is preparing

to launch or receive an attack. The concept of the guard in modern fencing as a position which in itself constitutes a defence against an attack in a particular 'line', is too new a concept to have any application to the style of fighting with which we are concerned in the theatre. An attack from quarte, for example, in modern foil fencing, delivered at the upper left quadrant of the target without a disengagement, requires no defensive movement on the part of the defender. The guard of quarte already adequately covers this quadrant against direct attack. But this is not true of the guard in Elizabethan rapier play, for example. In such play, any

27

attack requires a positive defensive move to counter it. If no defensive movement is made, that attack will succeed.

In theory, a very wide range of guard positions may be adopted, from which attacking or defensive movements can be launched. In practice, we need concern ourselves with only three guards. For convenience, we can classify these three guards as ATTACKING, DEFENSIVE and NEUTRAL.

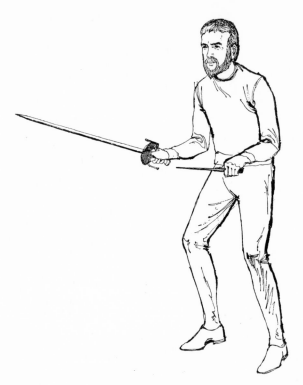

Attacking Guard

The general attitude here is one of aggression. The right foot is advanced in front of the left. The sword-arm is extended, with the point directed towards some part of the opponent's target. The dagger-arm is held close to the body so that the dagger, although remaining ready to receive any possible counter attack, does not hinder any forward movement of the sword. The position is illustrated on page 26.

Defensive Guard

The general attitude here is one of preparation to receive an anticipated attack. The right foot is withdrawn behind the line of the left. The sword-arm is held close to the body, although the point, as always, is directed towards the opponent. The dagger-arm is extended to receive a possible cut or thrust. The position is illustrated on page 27.

Neutral Guard

This is a compromise position. The feet are in line with one another. Both arms are held a little way in front of the body. It is a position most likely to be adopted at the beginning of a fight, or after a series of encounters which have failed to establish the superiority of either fighter. The position is illustrated on page 28.

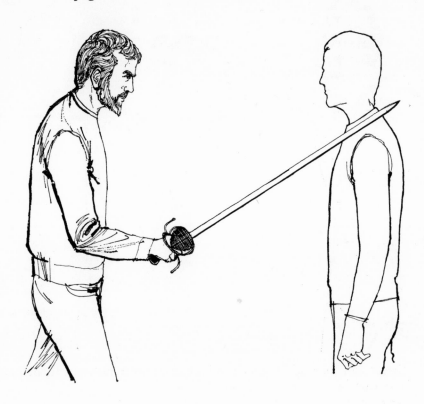

The Attack

The Cut

A cut is an attack made with either of the two sharpened edges of the blade. It can be made against any part of the opponent, but is probably most effective against the head and neck, the arms and the legs. It can be delivered crisply from the wrist or elbow, or, given an opponent taken completely off his guard, from the shoulder.

As with all attacking and defensive movements, the cut can be delivered as part of a general advance or retirement, or any other general body movement.

The Thrust

The thrust is an attack made with the point of the blade. It can be made against any part of the opponent, but will obviously be much more effective when directed at the head and body than when directed at arms and legs.

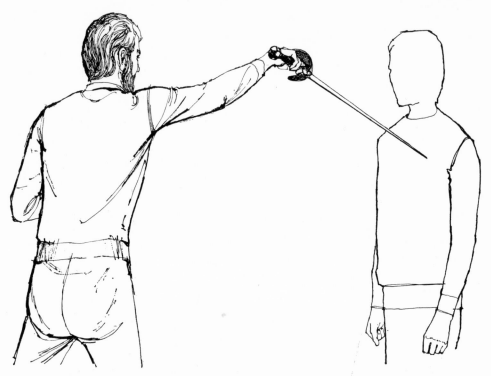

The thrust can be made without any general body movement, or it can be made as part of an advance or retirement.

The *lunge* in modern fencing is of little use in the theatre. Historically it did not appear until well after the Elizabethan period, the period which necessarily concerns us most closely. In its execution it requires the throwing back of the left hand, a movement which deprives an attacker of the chance of defending himself with that hand against any possible counterattack. A much more valuable movement for use in conjunction with the thrust, is *the pass*. We can visualize this most clearly if we imagine a fighter standing in the *Defensive Guard*, that is, with the left foot advanced in front of the right. He can launch an attack from this position by advancing the right foot so that it *passes* ahead of the left. If at the same time he extends the sword-arm ahead of him fully, the point of the sword can be made to travel at least eight feet. The move, apart from being in keeping with the style of fighting during the sixteenth and seventeenth centuries in particular, has the theatrical advantage of being visually clear to an audience. It is a move applicable to fighting of all periods, irrespective of weapon. It is, for example, as useful with a bottle or a bicycle chain as it is with a rapier.

The Punch

An attack with the blade—either cut or thrust—is certainly the gentleman's form of attack. But we must face the fact that in combat the instinct of self-preservation frequently transcends breeding. We cannot, in consequence, ignore blows which can most effectively be delivered with others parts of the sword.

The hilt of the sword can be used as a very formidable knuckle-duster, to deliver a punch to an opponent. The pommel—that lump of metal designed to counterbalance the weight of the blade—can be used to deliver a blow comparable with the butt stroke in bayonet fighting.

Nor, of course, are the possibilities of the punch restricted to the sword-hand. There is nothing in the rules of self-preservation that denies a fighter the use of his left hand. If that hand is wearing a mailed gauntlet, or carries a dagger or a stool or a buckler, so much the more effective. Nor is the punch restricted to the hands: a foot, an elbow or a knee could be used to deliver it. The head, particularly if clad in a metal helmet, can equally well be used to strike a blow on an opponent.

The Trip

The trip was taught as a legitimate move of personal combat by certain sixteenth-century Masters of Defence. It is certainly a possible move in combat, whatever weapons are being used. It might take one of several forms. The feet may simply be kicked from under an opponent, or he might be tripped by an extended foot in the course of a running attack. It might be executed by levering the opponent off balance over an outstretched leg, in the manner of a wrestling throw.

Alternatively, the weapon itself can be used in making the trip. In the case of the spear or quarterstaff, for example, a particularly effective trip can be accomplished by pushing the weapon between the opponent's legs and into the ground behind him. By lifting the butt of the weapon, the opponent can be lifted off his feet.

The Disarm

An opponent can be disarmed. The simplest, and probably most effective, way of doing this is to close with the opponent, grasp the hilt of his sword

31

and wrench it out of his hand by sheer force. A disarm that looks more spectacular can be made by parrying D (see the illustration on page 24) with the dagger, stepping towards the opponent with the right foot and at the same time slipping the blade of the sword under that of the opponent and sliding it up to the opponent's hilt. By pressing down with the dagger and at the same time lifting up sharply with the sword, the opponent's weapon can be prised out of his hand. But the method has its limitations. It requires surprise and very good timing. It is usually only completely effective against an opponent with a light grip on his weapon.

A disarm is possible, of course, by seizing the opponent's sword by the blade and wrenching it out of his hand. The move carries with it certain hazards in the case of an edged weapon. Only complete surprise, considerable luck—and the heaviest of gauntlets—will ensure any degree of success.

The Throw

Some weapons—the Roman *pilum* is one of them—are designed to be thrown at an opponent from a distance. But it is perfectly possible to throw any weapon and there are moments when such a move can be highly effective. The sword can be thrown. Equally, the defensive weapon—the dagger, the shield, the cloak—can be thrown. Again, surprise is an essential element in such a move.

The disadvantage of the throw, in the case of a weapon designed to be held in the hand, is obvious. If the move is unsuccessful, the thrower is left to face a counterattack virtually disarmed.

The Feint

The feint can best be classified as an attacking move, since its intention is to create an opening through which a genuine attack can be launched. It is in essence a pretence attack, designed to draw the opponent's defence to meet it. The drawing of the defence in one direction will necessarily leave other parts of the target undefended.

An attack on D, for example, might very well be preceded by a feint attack on A. The feint attack, if it has the appearance to the opponent of a genuine attack, will draw his defence up to receive it. Such a defensive movement will leave D undefended against the genuine attack.

Other movements which might be classified with the feint, are calculated more to upset the general rhythm of the opponent's fighting than to provide an opening for a specific attack. A sudden movement of any kind, which the opponent has not anticipated, will certainly fluster him. *The stamp* with either foot is a feint within this meaning. It has the effect of distracting the opponent's attention momentarily, and adding to his general tension. The stamp, executed suddenly and coinciding with the launching of an attack by the opponent, can render that attack abortive.

32

All movements that can be classified as feints, are essentially attacks on an opponent's psychology, rather than on his person.

Attacks with the left hand

In the case of a right-handed fighter, the weapon he carries in his right hand is the one he will use principally in attack. The weapon in his left hand will be used largely in defence. But there is no reason why on occasion the weapon in the left hand might not be used for attack. Suppose, for example, that an attack with the sword on D has been parried by the opponent with his dagger. The attacker's sword is therefore momentarily unavailable to him to continue the attack, yet the opponent, in making his parry, might have left himself exposed at E. In such circumstances the attacker can continue his attack by stepping forward with his left foot and striking his opponent at E with his dagger.

The Defence

The Displacement

This is one of the most valuable of defensive moves. It consists simply of moving the target out of the line of an attack: in a word, dodging. In the case of a cut to A, one can duck. In the case of a cut to F or G, one can jump over the attacking blade. In the case of a thrust at the foot, one can withdraw it.

More usefully, the displacement can be used in conjunction with a counterattack. Suppose one's left foot is advanced in the *Defensive Guard* described on page 28. It might present a target to an enterprising opponent. But if, as he thrusts at it, it is withdrawn, he is at an immediate disadvantage. The defender is free to strike him, with either cut or thrust, at A or in the upper back, and with cut on either arm or at F.

The Parry

There are, however, very many occasions when the target cannot be protected adequately by displacement. On these occasions, the opponent's sword must be met with either sword or dagger by the defender and positively carried off the line of the target. Such moves are known as *parries*. For the sake of convenience when we come later to plot a fight for the theatre, we can assume that in any guard position the points of the defender's sword and dagger are aimed at some point along the *centre line* of the opponent's target. We can then say that a parry is a movement of either sword or dagger that carries the attacking sword from the centre line, through a particular section of the target and subsequently off that

target. If we look again at the illustration of the target on page 24, we shall
see that *parry C sword* indicates a parry with the sword that carries an
attack on C from the centre line, through C and off the target. The opposing
sword in this case will pass outside the right arm. *Parry D dagger* describes
a parry with the dagger that carries an attack off the target through the
D section. In this case the attacking sword will pass outside the left hip.

Parry with the left hand

Because of the size and weight of the sword up to the early part of the
seventeenth century, the left hand was regarded as being principally
responsible for defence. And for more than a century after that period, it
was still regarded as an important factor in defence. Indeed, it would be
substantially true to say that as long as the use of the sword was taught for
purposes of personal combat, use of the left hand as part of the defence
employed by a fighter was regarded as important. Only when the use of the
sword becomes no more than a recreational activity in the gymnasium,
does the use of the left hand entirely disappear. If we are concerned with
sword play as combat, then we must regard the left hand as an important
part of defensive moves.

Parries with the left hand can be made with a range of weapons and
objects. The shield and the dagger are perhaps the most conventional of left-
handed weapons, but the cloak, wrapped a turn or two round the left
forearm, is equally effective in parrying an attack. The *case of rapiers*
involved the use of a rapier in the left hand as well as one in the right. For
purely defensive purposes, a light stool in the left hand can be as useful
as a dagger. A hat carried in the hand would certainly provide some
defence. The left hand wearing no more than a stout gauntlet can provide
a very effective defensive weapon. Certainly the bare left hand can be
used satisfactorily to guide an opponent's sword off the target.

Parry with the right hand

Angelo and others recommended the *circle parade* as being a general purpose
parry. It consisted simply in extending the arm and describing continuous
circles with the point of the sword. In theory it might pick up an attack
launched at any part of the target. In practice it might have had some
useful purpose in the confined space of an alleyway. Generally speaking,
however, circular parries seem not to have been found useful in the days of
serious personal combat. They have developed much more since the time
when fencing became a sport than they did in the grimmer days of the
duel. However much the circle parade and its precursors might have been
favoured by a particular fighter, we should regard the serious parry not as a
general defensive movement designed to protect the whole of the target at

once, but as a particular move designed simply to deflect a particular attack from a particular part of the target. During the periods with which the vast majority of fights in the theatre are concerned, the *simple parry* as it has been described on page 33 was the parry on which fighters most relied. The simple parry required a defender to contact an opponent's advancing blade with his own, and then, with a movement of the hand, carry that blade past his body.

The Counterattack

In general, the counterattack is best regarded as a form of attack, but there is certainly one form of counterattack that can be used principally as a defensive measure. Such a counterattack is one launched *at the same time* as the attack. Its intention is principally to break up such an attack; its secondary intention is to hit the attacker.

Broadly, we can divide the defence by counterattack into two forms. Suppose the opponent launches an attack, THRUST A. The defender can launch a simultaneous counterattack, THRUST E, and at the same time *displace* his body to the left. In this case he should strike the attacker at E, whilst the attacker's blade passes over his right shoulder. We can call this a *counterattack with displacement*. But suppose the opponent launches the same attack, THRUST A, and the defender decides to launch a simultaneous counterattack, also THRUST A. Unless he takes some additional action, he will walk on to the point of the attacker's sword. If, however, the defender contacts the attacker's blade in the course of his counterattack, and, by raising his sword hand guides the attacker's blade off the target, then his counterattack is likely to succeed whilst the attack itself passes above or to one side of his head. We can call such a movement a *counterattack with parry*. This is not to be confused with the *parry and riposte* of modern fencing. The *counterattack* is one movement, whereas the *parry and riposte* is best regarded as two.

There are other movements that we have already considered that can be used as counterattacks of defence. The *disarm*, executed by seizing the opponent's weapon and wrenching it from his hand, can be used as a counterattack where the movement coincides with the movement forward of the attacking blade. The *throw*, with either the sword or the dagger, can be used as a counterattack, if it is carried out simultaneously with an attack by the opponent, and if its intention is to thwart that attack.

Limitations of Analysis

This analytical consideration of the movements that are possible when two armed men fight one another, is useful up to a point. But of course a fight

35

has a continuity to it. It has a flow and a phrasing that cannot be usefully analysed. It has to be seen as one new movement arising out of a previous one and developing into a further one, all of which are being reacted to by an opponent. This continuity, this rhythm and phrasing, will be considered in more detail when we come to consider the creation of a theatrical fight in the next chapter.

4

The Fight in the Theatre

The fight in the theatre differs from the fight outside the theatre in intention. As we have seen, the intention of a fighter outside the theatre is to do physical injury to his opponent. The intention of the fighter in the theatre is to *appear* to do so. Nevertheless, all the movements possible in the *real* fight are equally possible in the *theatrical* fight. In the real fight these movements are largely spontaneous and unplanned. In the theatrical fight they must be planned and rehearsed as meticulously as any other part of the production. This planning requires some system for writing down the main movements of the fight.

A System of Notation

A complex notation of the moves that are possible in personal combat, is not necessary. Although fighting in the theatre has much in common with a dance routine, fighting and dancing are not the same thing. The dance is conducted within a much more rigidly prepared framework than is the fight. A complex form of notation, such as that devised by Laban, is no doubt invaluable for the choreographer and the dancer, but in the case of the fight it could provide a too-constricting framework for the actor engaged in fighting. We must remember, too, that a complex notation requires considerable study if it is to be mastered. A dancer can be expected to master such a notation, in the same way as a musician can be expected to master musical notation. But the actor is concerned with far more than simply the movements of a fight. It is unrealistic to expect an actor to master a complex notation that he is likely to use only infrequently. It is equally unnecessary for him to do so.

However, some very simple form of notation can be helpful to both fight arranger and actor. Such a notation need be no more than a brief outline of the main moves carried out by each fighter, reduced to shorthand form. Since modern fencing and the theatrical fight have almost nothing in common, no notation can usefully be based on the movements of modern fencing. It should be based, rather, on the movements that are possible and useful with a particular weapon.

37

Not only do the individual fighters make specific movements—cut, thrust, parry—but the fight itself moves. We can call such movements of the fight, *General Movements*, since they are carried out by both fighters. Such movements will be shown on the *Floor Plan*, rather than the individual *Fight Plot*, both of which will be dealt with in detail later.

Broadly speaking, there are only two General Movements with which we need concern ourselves. The first is a movement of the fight from one area of the stage to another. If the whole fight moves from a position on the stage that we have designated *Area 1* on the Floor Plan, to *Area 2*, we can represent this simply as:

Secondly, the fight may remain in one area, but turn about a central axis. Suppose the fighters remain facing one another, but move to their rights through a quarter of a circle, then we can represent this as:

Changes in the *pattern of levels* do not need a notation, since this pattern is dictated by the set pieces on the stage in the area where the fight is to be carried out.

SPECIFIC MOVEMENTS OF THE FIGHTERS

Foot Movements

In order to plot the *guards*, described on pages 27–29 and illustrated on pages 26–28, we need record only the foot positions. For this purpose, we should assume that we are looking down at our own feet. The Aggressive Guard, then, can be given this notation:

whilst the Defensive and Neutral Guards will appear respectively like this:

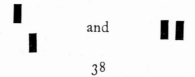

and

1 *Cup guard Rapier. Early 17th century. A reproduction*
2 *Shell guard Rapier. Early 17th century. A reproduction*

3 *Rapier with pierced shell*
   guards. Early 17th century.
   A reproduction

4 *Rapier with openwork guard.*
   Late 16th century.
   A reproduction

5 *Sword with knucklebow and side rings. 16th century. A reproduction*

6 *Hand and a half sword with front ring. Early 16th century. A reproduction*

7 *Ceremonial sword in rosewood.*
   Late 14th century.
   A reproduction

8 *Ceremonial sword in bleached*
   sycamore. Late 14th century.
   A reproduction

Foot movements from these guard positions can be indicated by elaborating this basic notation. The advancing of the right foot from the Aggressive Guard position, can be indicated in this way:

and the retirement of the right foot from the Neutral Guard position to the Defensive Guard, can be indicated like this:

A general advance of more than one step can be shown by placing this symbol below the foot notation:

In that case, this notation:

would indicate an advance of several steps, to the Aggressive Guard position. Similarly, a *general retirement* to a Defensive Guard position, can be shown in this way:

The Pass can also be shown as a variation of the basic foot notation:

This use of a hollow rectangle to indicate the position recently occupied by one of the feet, can also help to plot the *Feint by Stamping* and the *Displacement by Jumping*. They would appear respectively in this way:

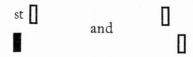

and

Other *Displacements* can use the same symbol, with the addition of an arrow, to indicate the direction of displacement. So this notation:

would indicate a displacement of the body to the right, by carrying the right foot further to the right from a Neutral Guard, and this:

would indicate a displacement to the left, by moving the right foot outside the left foot from an Aggressive Guard. A *Displacement by Ducking* can be indicated by placing a bar over the foot notation. This notation, then:

would indicate a displacement by ducking below the opponent's blade, from a Defensive Guard.

Movements of Attack

The two principal movements of attack, the *Cut* and the *Thrust*, can be represented respectively like this:

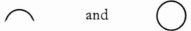

and

so that this notation:

$\widehat{A_r}$

would indicate a cut at the right side of the head, and:

would indicate a thrust at the left side of the chest.

This simple notation can be elaborated to indicate other forms of attack. This, for example:

$$\left(\text{pA}\right)$$

would show an *Attack by Punching*, launched with the left hand on the head. And this:

$$\left(\text{C}_t\right)$$

would show an *Attack by Throwing*, launched at the right side of the chest with the sword. Similarly, this:

$$\left(_l\text{D}\right)$$

would indicate a thrust attack on the left side of the abdomen, *with the left hand*.

We can indicate the *Feint* in the same way. To indicate a feint attack made by cutting with the dagger at the head, we can write down:

$$\overset{\frown}{_f\text{A}}$$

And this:

$$\left(\text{B}_f\right)$$

would indicate a feint attack made on the left side of the chest with a thrust of the sword.

The Trip is best indicated by the letters *tr*, followed by any necessary description in words, whilst the *Disarm* can be shown like this:

$$\underset{\sim\sim\sim}{\text{lev.}} \qquad \text{or} \qquad \underset{\sim\sim\sim}{\text{hand}}$$

The first symbol would show a disarm by leverage. The second would show a disarm by wrenching the opponent's weapon from him with the hands.

Movements of Defence
Defence by Displacement has already been dealt with as part of the Foot Movements.

The Parry can be represented by a single vertical line, so that this:

$$\big|$$

would indicate a parry made with the left hand, and this:

a parry with the right hand. There is no need, of course, to indicate in notation the area of the target that the parry is designed to protect, since this is already dictated by the direction of the attack.

Where it is thought necessary to indicate a *Counterattack*, launched against the opponent's attack, this can be done by underlining the relevant phrase of notation. So:

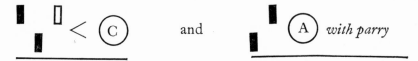

would indicate counterattacks, the first made by a displacement to the left combined with a thrust with the sword at the right side of the opponent's chest, and the second made by a thrust with the sword at the opponent's head in such a way as to deflect the opponent's attacking blade.

This particular notation of the counterattack, presents another problem. The first example might be read in this way: the defender moves his right foot and displaces his body to the left, *and then* attacks C with a thrust. This is not, of course, the case. We can indicate this unity of the movements in time, by a *phrasing mark* similar to that used in music. A more accurate notation of this move, then, would be:

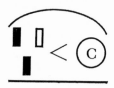

If, after the launching of the counterattack, the defender were to follow it up with a dagger-thrust to the right side of the abdomen, then the notation would appear like this:

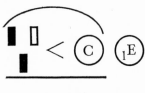

indicating that the symbols linked by the phrasing mark were to take place at the same time, whilst that following it took place afterwards.

A fight moves in a series of *phases*. The fighters close and attack one another, the attacks are parried, new attacks are launched and again parried; finally, the fighters break off the action before another sequence of attacks. These sequences of attack, or *phases* of the fight, should be shown in the fight plot for easy reference during rehearsal.

Rhythm, *timing* and *pauses* are all important aspects of the fight, but they need not be shown in notation. If necessary they can be shown on the fight plan in note form. Indeed, it is useful to limit any notation to the bare essentials and add any necessary details to it in terms of words. In fighting with the halberd, for example, it is better to describe a butt stroke to the left side of the head, as:

$$\overparen{A_1} \quad \textit{with butt}$$

than to invent any new notational symbol for this particular move.

The Director's Problem

The fight, in film, theatre or television, is essentially part of the total action of the plot. It cannot be seen as a separate entity. Ideally, then, the Director will be responsible for plotting and rehearsing the fight sequences as part of his total direction. In very few cases is the Director equipped to do this. Most directors will find it necessary to employ a *Fight Arranger*, a specialist who will be responsible for mounting the fights.

The problem for the Director is this: How is he to preserve a theatrical coherence and continuity, when part of the plot and rehearsal is out of his immediate control? Clearly he can only do this by insisting on the closest cooperation between himself and the fight arranger from the earliest stages of general plotting and rehearsal to the mounting of the finished production. He must discuss with the fight arranger his overall theatrical intention. He must make sure that his views on the characters within the play are known. He must have clear views on the theatrical significance of the fights, and share these views with the fight arranger. He must give the fight arranger a clear picture of the disposition of furniture, set-pieces and other actors during the fights. The fight arranger will need to know too, how the acting area is to be lit, what period feel the Director has in mind and what costumes are to be worn. He will want to discuss with the Director his first rough floor plan which shows the general movements of the fight, to see whether there is anything in it that conflicts with the Director's overall view.

43

The Fight Arranger's Problem

To some extent, the fight arranger's problem is that of the Director in reverse: how is he to mount a fight that forms a coherent part of the total theatrical intention? He must be more than a modern fencer, since only rarely will he be concerned with modern fencing in the theatre. He must be more than an arms historian, since he must know not only about the development of weapons but about their use as well. Most important, he must know about the theatre. He must know what limitations it places upon his activities. He must know the limitations and possibilities of an actor. He must understand the nature of an audience. In other words, he must be competent in overall direction since he is concerned not so much with fighting, but with the use of fighting to further a theatrical aim.

Granted a background of discussion with the Director, the fight arranger

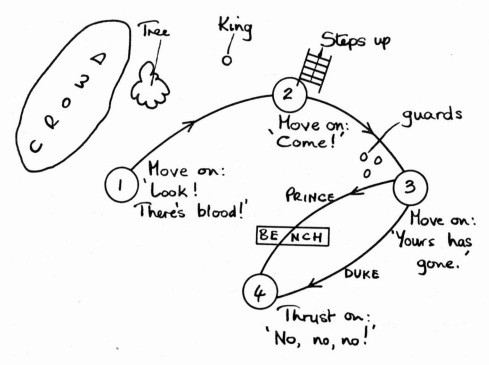

FLOOR PLAN for KING'S CARNIVAL showing 4 fight areas.
Starting position: ACT II sc i: p 39.
Script cue: 'So it's true then!'

can turn to the planning and rehearsal of the fight itself. His first move will probably be the preparation of a rough floor plan.

THE FLOOR PLAN

The floor plan is simply a bird's eye view of the whole acting area during the conduct of a fight. It will show the disposition of any furniture and set-pieces, together with the positions of other actors who are not directly concerned with the fight. It will show the various areas within which particular phases of the fight take place, and give cues from the script to show when the fight moves from one area to another.

A typical floor plan is shown opposite.

THE FIGHT PLOT

On the *fight plot* are marked the specific moves of each fighter, together with an indication of the fight area (shown on the floor plan) in which the moves take place, relevant cues from the script and the various phases into which the whole fight falls. The plot will take into consideration the Director's view of the play and of the characters within it, together with any specific statements in the script that are relevant to the conduct of the fight.

The fight plot can be worked out by the fight arranger before the first rehearsal, or it can be worked out during rehearsals with the actors. Usually a compromise is best. In that case, the fight arranger will come to the first rehearsal with a definite scheme, but one that is sufficiently elastic to allow alterations to be made to it as the need arises.

Part of the fight plot accompanying the floor plan shown on page 44, might look like this:

Fight Plot for 'King's Carnival'
Starting position: Act II, sc. i: p. 39.
Script cue: 'So it's true then!'

FIGHT AREA	SCRIPT	PHASE	DUKE	PRINCE
I	*Starting position*			
	Duke So it's true then!		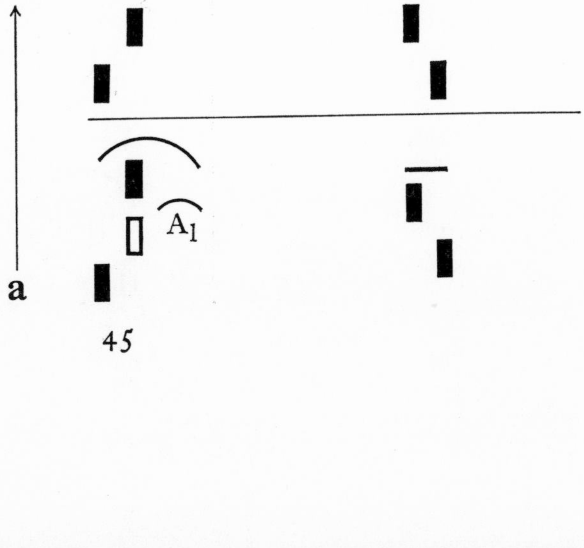 A_1	
		a		

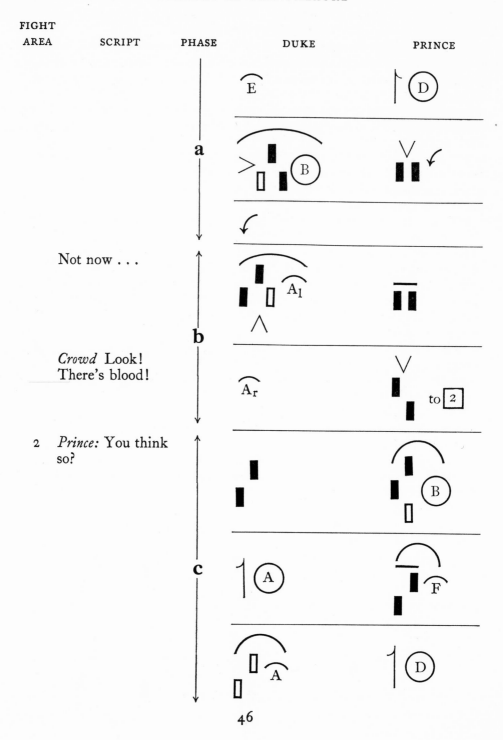

REHEARSING THE ACTORS

A fight is only the external manifestation of an inner attitude of aggression. The moves of a fight in the theatre will only be convincing to an audience, if an actor is using them to externalize a genuine feeling of aggression. The external movements of weapons have something of the same relationship to the actor as has his make-up. No amount of highly skilled make-up will age an actor who has not already identified himself with the feelings and attitudes of age. In the same way, the fight must be initiated within the actor, not within the sword. The first approach to the fight, then, must be the creation within the actor of an inner attitude of aggression. This might be done through improvisation, as well as through the normal processes of direction.

Given this inner attitude, the specific moves through which it will be made manifest to an audience, can be *walked through*. This *walking through* consists essentially of carrying out the moves in slow motion. Initially, the walk through will establish whether the projected moves in the fight plot actually work. Later, repeated walk throughs are necessary not only to develop the actors' skill in using them, but to fix the moves in their memories. In theory, it is possible for an actor highly experienced in theatrical fighting to memorize the moves from a notation. In practice, this method is not even worth considering. During the repeated walk throughs, the fight should be rehearsed in its *phases* rather than in its entirety. Only when the first phase can be walked through with some assurance, should the next phase be introduced.

This business of memorizing a series of complex movements may be difficult for some actors. The fight arranger can help considerably here by introducing a good deal of repetition of movement sequences, varying their rhythm and timing so that they are not recognizable as repetitions to an audience. The sequence to be repeated might appear, for example, like this:

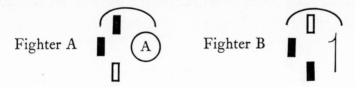

The first repetition would be this:

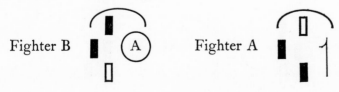

The fighters, having each completed an attack which has been parried, move round one another in an anticlockwise direction through 90°, looking for an opening. The two attacks are then repeated, with Fighter B initiating the process this time:

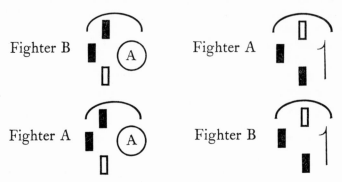

Further repetitions are possible by substituting *cuts* on the part of one fighter, for *thrusts*:

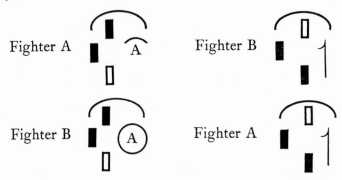

Equally, the same general movement pattern can be repeated, varying only the target area that is attacked:

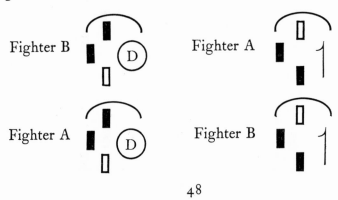

Such repetitions make the memorizing of a fight by the actors, a much simpler business. This is a factor of extreme importance, since any lapse of memory during performance means that the actors are no longer following the predictable patterns of a well rehearsed activity, but are left to improvise with no more protection than their own fighting skill and the costumes they are wearing.

The initial stages of rehearsal are best conducted with ash sticks fitted with some basketwork protection for the hands. Practice weapons, suitable particularly for the rapier and dagger fight can be made of bamboo. For additional protection they should be fitted with rubber ferrules. These are heavy enough to give the feel of production weapons, and cumbersome enough to prevent an actor who is skilled in modern fencing resorting to such theatrical irrelevancies as the *finger counter-parry*. Throughout all stages of rehearsal, of course, face masks must be worn to protect the eyes.

As we have seen, the initial stages of rehearsal are taken up mainly with the learning of the moves to the point where they become automatic. Even here, though, the final appearance of the fight to the audience should be borne in mind. A fight arranger, sitting six feet from the actors, will have no difficulty in seeing a fast cut to the head. Such a move, however, might be entirely missed by a member of the audience seated a hundred feet away. The particular move needs pointing by some general body movement accompanying it. The audience needs, as it were, a large general movement to focus its attention on the more specific movement that it is expected to register.

Later rehearsals will be concerned with variations in rhythm and speed, designed to increase and decrease the theatrical tension of the fight. They will be concerned with the general increase in speed of the movements that initially were only walked through. This increase in speed must never be at the expense of accuracy of movement. Indeed, as a general principle it can be said that accuracy is more important than speed, and that the fastest speed at which any fight can be fought is never more than that at which the movements can be executed with complete accuracy. In any case, the speed of a fight in the theatre need never be very great. The tension and excitement of a fight arises more from the quality of the acting than from a brilliant display of skill in the technical handling of weapons. Speed beyond a certain point will make the movements of a fight incomprehensible to an audience.

These later rehearsals should, of course, be carried out with the actual production weapons. They should be carried out in costume well before performance, since certain types of costume can be much more confining than rehearsal dress. Equally, the fight should be tested under the lighting conditions planned for the performance, well in advance of that performance.

The rehearsals should include practice in wearing the weapons, apart from using them in the fight.

The Weapons of Theatrical Combat

The weapons used in theatrical fighting need to be specially designed for the purpose. It has been established earlier that neither the authentic weapon nor the weapons used in modern fencing have any useful place in theatrical combat. The most important factor in the design of theatrical weapons is one of safety. No weapon, of course, can be entirely safe whilst remaining a weapon, but it is possible to effect useful compromises on this point. The blade, for example, should have no sharp edge to it. The point should be flattened so that penetration is almost impossible. A compromise is possible, too, between the need for safety and the need for a certain historical accuracy in appearance. The openwork guard of the authentic late sixteenth-century rapier can be filled in to some extent, to provide greater protection for the hand. Alternatively, a solid or pierced cup guard can replace the openwork guard, without any serious loss of historical accuracy in appearance.

Weight is an important consideration in the theatre, though not to the extent that has at times been suggested. A compromise is possible here by using such new materials as hard aluminium alloy for bucklers and rapier cup guards, and by paying particular attention to the balance of a weapon. But the use of new materials in the manufacture of theatrical weapons is limited. Experiments have been carried out in the manufacture of weapons from plastics. But no actor who picks up such a weapon believes for a moment that it could, by any stretch of the imagination, be used to slaughter Macbeth or stab Laertes to death. And unless the actor can believe, how is he to project credibility to his audience? Equally, blades have been made from alloys of aluminium. They are credible in appearance, they have some of the feel of a genuine weapon to the actor, and they are possibly safer in use. But an audience has heard steel touch steel. It has an expectation of the sound it will hear when Hamlet's blade meets Laertes' for the first time. Aluminium on aluminium sounds quite different from steel on steel. The expectation of the audience is not fulfilled and the illusion of reality is destroyed. It is unfortunate that research, for example that conducted by Swords of York Ltd., has produced no alternative as far as blades are concerned to sword steel heat-treated to give a Brinnell hardness reading of 2·95–3·2, measured with a 10 mm ball and load of 3,000 kg. It is, nevertheless, a fact.

In the matter of choice of weapons to be used in a particular fight, the relationship of fight arranger to designer has come into increasing prominence in the British theatre during recent years. Naturally enough, the designer wishes to preserve a design unity throughout the production. Such a unity necessarily includes the weapons used in the fight. But there have been many productions recently that indicate the subservience of the fight arranger to the designer in the choice of weapons. Weapons have clearly been designed and produced for the sake of their appearance, without any consideration of whether they can be used by actors in the conduct of a fight. In the Royal Shakespeare Company's production of the Wars of the Roses series at Stratford on Avon during the 1965 season, swords were used with blades of mild steel. This in itself is unimportant. But what is vitally important is that when such blades inevitably bent in the course of serious combat, the audience, instead of being held in a state of increasing tension, was reduced to a bubble of laughter. Final decisions on the choice of fighting weapons must be left to the fight arranger, under the overall supervision of the Director.

The Fight in Actor Training

All serious actor training includes a good deal of general movement work. This, of course, is essential, since movement is the external basis of the actor's work. A good deal of movement training is concerned with dance, both free dance and such formalized dance as classical ballet. Many actors in their training are taught the specific movements of such dances as the *pavane*, the *minuet* and the *tarantella*. All this general and specific movement training forms an admirable basis for the training of actors in the fight.

Most serious actor training includes modern fencing, in particular foil fencing. As a tool for increasing the precision of movement, and for developing timing, poise and physical control, modern fencing can be invaluable. But as a basis for fighting in the theatre, it has very limited application.

Very little time is given at present in actor training, to the business of the use of violence in the theatre. This is surprising. For every once that he is asked to dance the *pavane*, the actor is likely to be asked to fight fifty times. It is impossible for an actor to appear with any regularity in the classic plays of the British theatre, without being required frequently to show skill in the handling of arms. A glance at the contemporary film and television scene gives ample evidence that this tradition is a continuing one.

The training of actors for work in the contemporary theatre must include some work in the use of physical violence, as part of the general training in movement. Acrobatics should certainly form part of this training. Training in *quarterstaff* would give the actor experience in the use of all staff weapons. Training in Elizabethan *broadsword and buckler* play and play with *rapier and dagger* would give him experience with the theatre's classical weapons. Some experience is necessary with the *small sword* of the eighteenth century. Certainly, if he is to be properly equipped to enter film and television, he should have had some instruction in the moves of the *modern roughhouse*.

It is fashionable to decry violence without examining its nature as an undeniable aspect of life. Certainly, any examination of the nature of drama will discover conflict at its core. Violence is this core of drama given physical manifestation. When we consider the non-physical conflict in the plays of Ibsen and Strindberg, for example, conflict resulting in the total destruction of one human being by another, we cannot but wonder whether it is not ultimately more corrosive, more utterly corrupting, than a sword thrust through the breast. An actor trained to handle conflict in only its more respectable manifestations is an actor trained for only a part of his job in the theatre.

5

Greece & Rome

Background

It is impossible to say with any degree of certainty what personal combat looked like in the days of the classic civilizations. A good deal can be deduced from the art of the period, from decorations on vases, from friezes, and from such detailed pieces as Trajan's Column. But we are left to build such images into a continuity ourselves.

More profitably, we can look at what remains of the weapons themselves. Reconstructions of them, in the hands of anyone accustomed to handling weapons, give us a much clearer idea of their possibilities and limitations. The 18-foot spear of the Macedonian *phalangite*, for example, was clearly not intended for throwing. The *gladius*—the Roman short sword—is of little use for parrying.

The Weapons of Greece

The Sword

In the early Greek period, the sword was comparatively long. The blade was narrow and pointed and was clearly used more for thrusting than for cutting. As the period advanced, the sword diminished in length. It may have been that with the development of body armour, something more rigid was necessary to effect penetration. The sword of the *hoplite*—the heavily-armoured foot soldier of the Greek city states—had a blade length of no more than 18 to 24 inches. It cannot be regarded as his principal weapon. By contrast, the *peltasts*—light infantry used for skirmishing—tended to keep still to the longer sword. The typical sword of the period is, however, short. The leaf-shaped blade, characteristic of the earlier years, gives way to a blade with parallel edges.

The Spear

Throughout the period, the spear appears to have been the principal weapon of attack. In the case of the *hoplite*, it was a stout pike measuring between 6 and 9 feet in overall length, clearly unsuitable for throwing. From the fourth century B.C., the length of the spear increased. It appears in some cases, perhaps not typical, to have been a two-handed weapon of some 17 or 18 feet in length.

By contrast, the spear of the light infantry was a throwing weapon. It was light in weight and measured some 3 to 5 feet. Whereas the *hoplite* would carry only a single spear for thrusting, the *peltast* would carry a number of throwing spears.

The Shield

Some form of shield was carried by all fighting men. In the Homeric, Minoan and Mycenaean periods, the characteristic shield was of the figure-of-eight shape, known frequently as the *Boeotian* type. It was some 3 to 5 feet in length, and about 14 inches wide at the waist. Its construction—of ox-hide, with a metal rim and central boss—must have made it extremely heavy. A stout leather strap over the left shoulder supported most of the weight, and any manoeuvring of it was done with the left hand which held a grip at the back of the shield. There are examples in the period of a large round shield measuring some 3 feet in diameter.

The shield most characteristic of the hoplite was oval, with an average length of 4 feet and a width of about 18 to 24 inches. It was probably still supported by a shoulder strap and manoeuvred with the left hand when necessary, but there is evidence of the replacement of the shoulder strap by an arm-loop fitted to the back of the shield, in addition to the grip. This would throw the whole weight on the left arm. It would increase the manoeuvrability of the shield, but must be taken to indicate a reduction in its weight. In this later period, the large round shield with a diameter in excess of 2 feet, is also common.

The round shield seems to have been the principal form of defence for the light infantry. It was carried on the left forearm by an arm-loop and grip. Later in the period, it diminished in size. A typical light shield of this later period might measure about 18 inches in diameter. Such a shield is highly manoeuvrable. Painted devices appeared on the shield. Initially these devices must have been personal, but later, perhaps, regimental.

The Bow and the Sling

The bow was part of the equipment of the light infantry. In length it was perhaps a little over 3 feet. There are accounts in Xenophon of its being used effectively as a means of mass attack from a distance against formations of heavy infantry, but the fact that the archer remained essentially part of the skirmishing and harassing force and not part of the main body of hoplites indicates certain crucial limitations in the bow of the period.

The sling, like the bow, is another weapon for projecting a missile over a distance. As with the bow, it seems to have been effective in the general

9 *Sword: 14th century.*
   A reproduction

10 *Sword: 13th century.*
    A reproduction

11 *Sword: 11th century.
A reproduction*

12 *Roman Legionary's sword: the
Gladius. A reproduction*

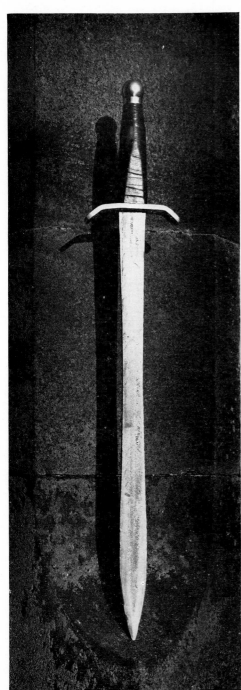

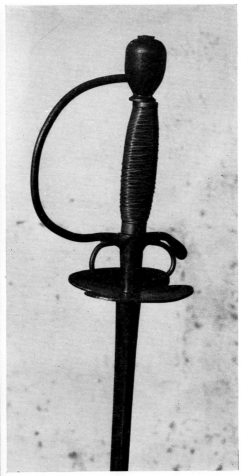

Greek Short sword.
A reproduction
13

Above *small sword hilt:* 18th
century. *A reproduction*
14

15 Above *broad sword with side rings. Early 16th century. A reproduction*

16 *Broad sword hilt with side ring and knucklebow. A reproduction*

harassment of the main body of enemy forces before they came to grips with the hoplites, but the slingers never formed part of the main attacking body.

The Weapons of Rome

The weapons of Rome have much in common with those of the later Greek period.

The Sword

The most effective, and most typical, sword of the Roman period was the *gladius*, the principal weapon of the heavy-armed infantryman, the *legionary*. Made of iron, it had a blade length of some 20 to 24 inches, and a width of at least 2 inches. The last quarter of the blade tapered evenly to a point. The grip, usually of wood, had indentations for the fingers.

Throughout the period, a longer thrusting sword—the *spatha*—was used by the auxiliary soldier.

The Dagger

A dagger, with a blade length of 8 to 9 inches, was carried from the belt. If had the appearance of a miniature *gladius*. It was probably regarded as a general purpose tool, rather than a weapon. Its use in fighting must have been very limited.

The Spear

The *hasta*, the stout thrusting spear comparable to the weapon carried by the hoplite in Greece, although remaining part of the equipment of some auxiliary troops, was replaced for the legionary by the *pilum*.

The *pilum* was a light, well balanced throwing spear, about 7 feet in length. Of this length, at least 2 feet was of round iron, fixed to the wooden shaft by a metal socket. One disadvantage of any throwing weapon is that it can be picked up by the enemy and thrown back. In the case of the *pilum*, two methods were introduced to overcome this. In the first method, the long metal head was fixed to the shaft by a wooden pin. On impact, this pin was sheared, so that the head became detached from the shaft. The second method consisted of making the metal shaft of soft iron, whilst leaving the point hardened. On impact, the metal shaft bent and had to be straightened before the weapon was again serviceable. The virtue of both methods was that spent *pila* could be recovered from the battlefield after the action, and made serviceable again with very little effort.

Certain auxiliary troops carried a light thrusting spear, the *iaculum*.

The Shield

The *clipeus*, a light, round shield following logically from the round shield of Greece, was gradually replaced by the much more substantial *scutum*. Certain auxiliaries, however, did retain a small round buckler, the *parma*.

The *scutum* had two main shapes. In its oval form, it measured between 3 and 4 feet in length, and up to 24 inches in width at the waist. It had a rim of iron and a deep central boss of iron or bronze. It carried painted emblems which were probably regimental.

The later, and probably more typical, form of the *scutum* was rectangular. It was deeply concave on the inside, like a half cylinder, so that when carried it gave protection not only to the front of the body but to much of the sides as well. It was similar in size to the oval *scutum* and was re-inforced by the same iron rim and large boss. It carried similar painted devices.

Both forms of the *scutum* must have been very heavy, and it seems probable that a leather strap passing from the shield over the left shoulder spread a good deal of this weight to the body of the wearer. The left hand, holding a grip in the centre, or to one side, of the back of the shield, could be used to carry out whatever limited manoeuvres were necessary for full defence.

The Bow and the Sling

These weapons were still used principally for skirmishing. They seem never to have formed an integral part of the weapons of the main infantry forces.

The Real Fight in Greece and Rome

The massed battle on the Grecian plain or in the open valleys of Gaul, is not too difficult to visualize. We have accounts of such battles in writings of the period, and we have the visual evidence on such monuments as Trajan's Column. Equally important, we have a few remains of the weapons that were used. We can see the way in which the archers and slingers could be used to harass and disorganize a mass of heavy-armed infantrymen in slow advance. We can see how light infantry, wearing almost no body armour, could move quickly upon a flank, throw their javelins, and retire untouched. This overall view is important if we are to set the individual fighting man in context. It is, of course, important in itself if we are concerned with the filming of this background. But in the end our main concern must be with the individual himself. We need to try to imagine his behaviour when face to face with a single opponent. And this is a good deal more difficult. In order to attempt it, let us confine ourselves to three separate fighting men. The *light infantryman*, the *hoplite* and the *legionary*.

The Light Infantryman

Suppose we look for a moment at a typical soldier of the light infantry, armed with three or four throwing spears and carrying a circular shield on his left arm. At his left side he carries a long sword of bronze or iron. The spears are about 5 or 6 feet in length. The shield has a diameter of 30 inches and is carried with the left arm thrust through an arm-loop and the hand holding a fixed grip on the right side of the shield. The sword, hanging either from his waist belt or from a strap over his right shoulder, has a blade length of 27 or 30 inches. He wears a short tunic and perhaps a felt hat on his head. If he is fortunate he may wear a padded jerkin on top of the tunic, but he carries no metal armour.

The Attack and the Defence   As he moves in with his companions on the flank of a *phalanx* of heavy-armed infantry, he carries one of his throwing spears ready in his right hand. The rest of his spears are held, together with the shield-grip, in his left hand.

At a distance of perhaps 200 yards, when he is already exposed to the fire of archers and slingers, he breaks into a run. His shield is raised to protect his head and body from falling missiles. At a distance of 100 yards he prepares to throw his first spear into the main body of infantry. At 70 or 80 yards he releases this spear in a high trajectory, whilst still on the run. He plucks the next spear from his left hand and throws it. Each throw will, of course, hold up momentarily his progress forward, so that he will have discharged all his throwing weapons when he is still some 50 yards from the main body of the enemy.

It would be disastrous for him to close with heavy-armed infantry, armed only with a sword. So, after the discharge of his last spear, he turns from the attack and withdraws as quickly as possible beyond the range of arrows and sling-shot.

Against the *hoplite* or the *legionary* such a man would have little chance of survival. His only advantage is his mobility. But what are his tactics likely to be against another light infantryman? Both have discharged their spears and now close on one another armed with swords and round shields. A fight between two such combatants must have been similar to that between two Elizabethans, armed with the short sword and buckler, discussed in chapter 8. Mobility is an important part of both attack and defence. Attacks are made with both the cutting edge and the point of the blade.

In defence, the padded jerkin provides some protection against the cut, though little against the thrust. The main defence is with the shield, sufficiently light to be manoeuvrable, yet large enough to protect a substantial area of the body. Mobility is a great advantage over a less mobile opponent, though no advantage over one who is equally mobile.

The Hoplite

The heavy-armed infantryman forms the core of the typical fighting force. He wears a helmet with protection for the nose, cheeks, and much of the upper part of the face, together with breastplate and bronze greaves. He is further burdened with a large shield. He carries a short sword at his left side, suspended from a waist belt or from a separate strap over his right shoulder. As his main weapon of attack, he carries a substantial thrusting spear. The weight of his equipment in battle has been estimated at more than 70 pounds.

The Attack and the Defence   In essence the *hoplite* is slow-moving. When organized in the *phalanx*—the solid formation of men advancing shoulder to shoulder and several ranks deep—he operates like a tank. Against the arrows and sling-shot of the enemy skirmishers, he is well protected by his armour and shield. Only when he is in direct physical contact with the enemy can be begin to fight.

In direct attack, he is too hemmed in by his companions and too weighted with armour to engage in any subtle play with his substantial thrusting spear. He holds the spear horizontally as the clash of bodies becomes imminent, the butt under his armpit. In the last second he seeks out an enemy body through a chink in the opposing shield wall, and lets the momentum of his advance carry the spear forward and on to the target. If his spear finds the target, he withdraws it and continues to advance over his enemy, his spearpoint directed towards the next immediate target. If, on the other hand, he is wounded himself, then his place is taken by a comrade from the rank behind him.

If he becomes isolated from his immediate comrades in the *phalanx*, he can use his spear with a good deal more freedom. It is not too unwieldy to be used as a single-handed thrusting weapon. Used as a two-handed weapon, it is effective, though its movements are restricted by the need to support the shield with the left hand. In isolation, the hoplite is at his most effective if freed from his shield. He can then use his spear as a pointed polearm, whilst his body armour still provides him with considerable protection.

The hoplite, robbed of his spear, must fall back on his sword. Facing the light infantryman with this weapon, he is at a disadvantage. The mobility of the light infantryman allows him to avoid any counterattacks launched by the hoplite, whilst picking his own time for attacks. The light infantryman's longer sword makes it possible for him to strike whilst still being out of range of the hoplite's own sword. Given two fighters of equal merit, the mobility of the one will prove a greater advantage to him than will defensive armour to the other.

The Legionary

Much that has been said about the hoplite is applicable to the legionary of Rome. He wears a helmet, with cheek pieces. A bar at the front of the helmet gives additional protection to the forehead and face against a cut downwards. The back of the helmet has a half-moon extension in metal to protect the neck. He carries a *scutum* and wears defensive armour consisting of breast and backplates and sets of flexible metal straps to protect the shoulders. Beneath the armour is a stout tunic which gives protection from chafing by the armour. From a waist belt he carries a dagger over his left hip. Suspended from a belt passing over the left shoulder, he carries the *gladius*, its pommel on a level with his right armpit so that the weapon does not impede him when moving quickly, nor interfere with the movements of his shield arm. He carries a *pilum* in his right hand, and possibly two additional ones in his left.

The Attack and the Defence   As with the *hoplite*, the *legionary* moves in mass formation, each soldier standing so close to his neighbour as to present an almost continuous shield wall to the enemy. The discharge of *pila* takes place at comparatively close range, since the chaos that this discharge is calculated to cause amongst the enemy front line needs to be capitalized at once. No time interval must elapse between it and the first physical contact, that will allow the enemy to reform. Thirty yards is certainly a most effective killing range with the *pilum*. Those *pila* which penetrate the opposing shields, will bend. No man is at his most effective when trying to defend himself with 7 feet of metal and wood shaft sticking out of his shield.

After the discharge of *pila*, the legionary draws his *gladius*—either upwards past his right shoulder, or outwards having first turned the scabbard horizontally across his lower chest—and moves forward as quickly as his weight of equipment will allow, to take advantage of an already confused enemy line. He uses the *gladius* rather like a bayonet, not to cut at an enemy whose head and shoulders may be well protected, but to thrust below the line of his chest armour.

The legionary is at a similar disadvantage to that of the hoplite when isolated from the rest of his formation. His shield and body armour make him slow-moving by comparison with the light infantryman. The *pilum* cannot be used effectively as a thrusting spear because it is constructed to bend on first impact, so that, unlike the hoplite, he cannot make himself more effective by dispensing with his shield.

But in mass formation both hoplite and legionary are almost unstoppable. And such a mass formation is not restricted to use in the *phalanx*. The *tortoise*—the use of overlapping shields raised over the crouched backs of an advancing formation to protect it from attack from above—is an effective formation in attacks on fortifications where missiles are likely to be hurled down from above.

The Fight in the Theatre

If we are to bring Greek or Roman heavy infantry into the theatre, we must use them *en masse*. Act V sc. iv of *Julius Caesar* and Act I sc. iv of *Coriolanus* clearly demand such treatment. The *Coriolanus* scene in particular, gives scope for mass battle movements before Corioli. The cry of Martius on the entry of the army of the Volsces, is clearly made to a mass formation of heavy infantry:

> They fear us not, but issue forth their City.
> Now put your shields before your hearts, and fight
> With hearts more proof than shields.
> Advance, brave Titus:
> They do disdain us much beyond our thoughts,
> Which makes me sweat with wrath. Come on my fellows:
> He that retires, I'll take him for a Volsce,
> And he shall feel mine edge.

There are, however, occasions when two men alone face one another. To saddle them with the equipment of the heavy infantryman would be to rob the fight of much of its theatrical significance. The long sword and circular shield of the light infantryman would be more suitable for the Troylus–Diomedes fight (Act V, sc. iv, *Troylus and Cressida*) for example. Long sword and circular shield are certainly more in keeping with the style of fighting that Shakespeare had in mind when he wrote the play, if we are to judge from internal evidence—Elizabethan broadsword and buckler fighting in fact.

A Plot for a 'Caesar' Fight

At the beginning of Act V, sc. iv of *Julius Caesar*, we find Brutus, young Cato, Lucilius 'and others' engaging a detachment of soldiers from the forces of Antony and Octavius. A full plot for the fight as a whole, would require a separate plot for each fight, and then the coordination of all of them into a total battle sequence. It is sufficient here if we look at one of these fights, that between young Cato and his opponent.

A soldier of the armies of Antony and Octavius runs on to the stage in retreat. He carries a large circular shield and two *pila*. He wears a long sword at his left side. He has a helmet and a padded jerkin. Centre stage he stops, turns and throws a *pilum*. He retreats a further step and throws his second *pilum*. Cato enters. He wears a helmet and light body armour and carries a long sword. The last *pilum* has embedded itself firmly in his shield. He tries to shake it loose and then pull it out with his sword hand, but without success. His opponent, seeing Cato's difficulty, draws his sword and rushes at him. Cato throws aside the shield:

SCRIPT	PHASE	CATO	OPPONENT

Brutus Yet, countrymen, O, yet hold up your heads!

Cato (*discards shield*): What bastard doth not?

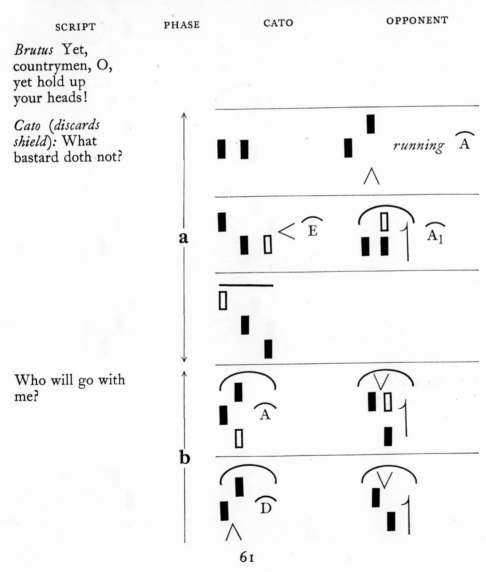

Who will go with me?

SCRIPT	PHASE	CATO	OPPONENT

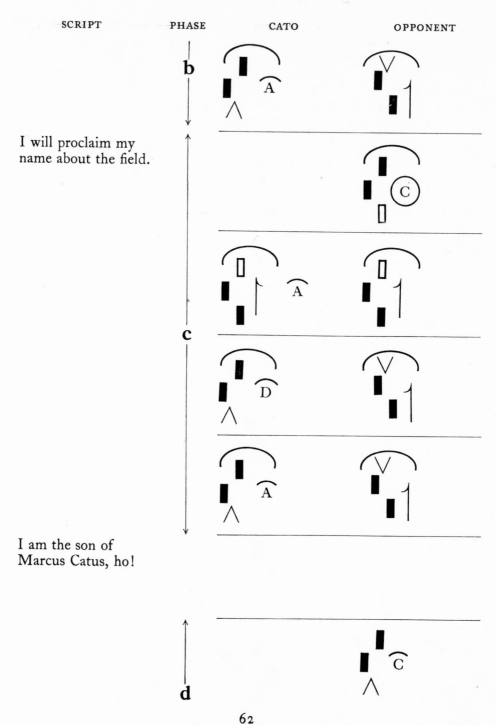

I will proclaim my
name about the field.

I am the son of
Marcus Catus, ho!

SCRIPT   PHASE   CATO   OPPONENT

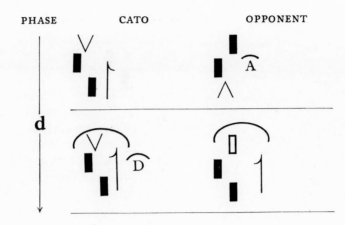

A foe to tyrants,
and my country's
friend; I am the
son of Marcus
Catus, ho!

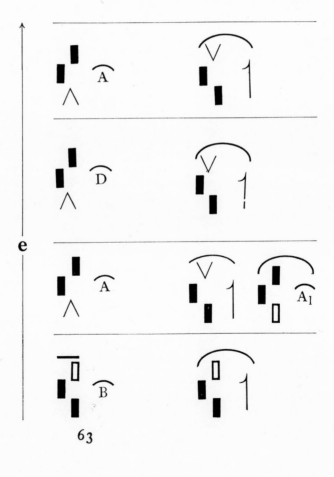

Brutus And I am
Brutus, Marcus
Brutus, I; Brutus
my country's
friend; know me
for Brutus! (*Exit
Brutus.*)

SCRIPT	PHASE	CATO	OPPONENT

He is struck in C and falls.

e

Three legionaries *move, shoulder to shoulder, on* Cato *and stab him with* gladii.

6

Huns, Goths, Vikings, Normans

Background

We think perhaps of the Roman phalanx of legionaries as a formation of such mechanical precision, that the individual soldier almost ceases to exist. He is no more than a highly-disciplined cog in a vast military machine. If we were to make a similar generalization about warfare during the period of the great migrations westwards of the tribes of Asia and central Europe, and during the period of the Vikings and the early Normans, we might well conclude that they were periods in which the individual fighting man was of more importance than the well-disciplined machine.

Both generalizations are likely to be inaccurate in many cases, but each contains a substantial element of truth. The weapons of these periods give far more freedom of action to the individual fighting man, than do those of the Roman legionary, and the literature and art of the period support the view that individual skill, courage and aggression, were the deciding factors of a battle, rather than mass discipline.

The Sword

The development of the sword during the period is one of a gradual increase in size. The *gladius* of the Roman legionary had an overall length of perhaps 24 inches, whereas the average sword of the Viking and Norman period had an overall length of 36 to 39 inches. Coupled with this increase in size was an increase in quality of workmanship, leading to a better balance of weapons. At the same time, there was a gradual simplification of the sword; the beauty of later swords lies not in their decoration but in their simplicity of line. The sword of the later years of the period was of its kind a quite perfect fighting weapon.

This is a vast period out of which to select a typical sword suitable for use in the theatre. If we were to do so, then we could describe such a sword as having an overall length of 33 to 36 inches, a wooden grip perhaps bound with leather, a simple cross guard or iron and a flat or domed iron pommel. The point of balance would be about an inch below the cross guard in the direction of the point. The double-edged blade would be capable of both cut and thrust.

The Sax

The *sax* is a weapon that appears throughout the period. It differed from the sword in two ways: in the first place it was rather shorter in length, in the second place it was a single-edged weapon. Existing remains of saxes suggest that the weapon could be used for both the cut and the thrust.

The Short Sax

This was a much shorter version of the long sax. It is best regarded as an early form of dagger. It was pointed and single-edged.

The Spear

The spear appears in various forms throughout the period. Although lighter spears were used for throwing, either with the hand or with the help of a string attachment, the heavier thrusting spear was probably more favoured. Some of these thrusting spears reached considerable lengths and could best be used as two-handed weapons.

The typical spear of the period, for theatrical purposes, can be described as a thrusting weapon of some 7 feet in length that could be used with either one or two hands.

The Axe

Although the axe was used throughout the period, it came fully into its own during the later years. Early axes appear to have been light in weight and some were used for throwing. But the Viking axe was a substantial weapon with a curved blade some 12 inches in length and a handle some 3 to 4 feet in length. This axe and the great axe of the Normans, with its handle up to 5 feet in length, was almost certainly a two-handed weapon. Used as such, the damage it could do was immense.

The Shield

The principal shield shape was circular. It varied in size from about 24 inches to the 36 inches of many Viking shields. It was supported on the left arm by a loop and a hand grip. In the case of larger and heavier shields, the main weight seems to have been borne by a leather strap from the shield which passed over the shoulder. Such additional support would be necessary in the case of a shield that had to be slung out of the way by a fighter using a two-handed weapon.

The circular shield was flat in side view and made of wooden planking fixed together by wooden battens on the reverse side. The face bore decorations of a personal nature. It was fitted with a large central boss of iron and had additional metal protection on the face in the form of studs or a circular band at the periphery.

66

Two other forms of shield need to be noted. Early in the period a rectangular shield, slightly 'waisted', was in use. The *Battersea Shield* is a beautiful example of this shape. At the end of the period the Norman 'kite' shield appears. This was a shield some 42 inches in height, principally for use on horseback because of the additional protection it gave to the lower left side of the body and the upper part of the left leg. But the 'kite' shield was by no means restricted to use on horseback. The *Bayeux Tapestry* has many examples of its use on foot.

The Bow

Archers were used extensively throughout the period, although their position was usually auxiliary to the main forces. The bow remained comparatively short. Mounted archers were used for skirmishing and the use of mass archers was perhaps a decisive factor in the outcome at Hastings.

The Real Fight

We might sense the nature of real combat of the period, in the way that we must for theatre purposes, if we imagine a small detachment of a Viking raiding party in action. Our first view of the detachment gives the impression of a group of perhaps twenty men, each equipped in much the same way. They wear helmets and byrnies—the shirt of mail. All wear swords slung at their left sides from waist belts, and all carry large circular shields. Some carry stout thrusting spears. Others carry battle axes.

The Attack and the Defence

They move towards their opponents in no particular formation, giving voice to various calls to Odin and other northern Gods, perhaps as much to work themselves up to a pitch of aggression where thought for personal safety ceases to exist, as to terrify the enemy.

As they move closer, we can see individual differences. Most wear rather simple conical helmets; one or two wear more elaborate ones with brims to protect face and neck and a cockscomb of iron running from the back towards the front. Many of the byrnies cover only the upper part of the arms, and the back and chest as far as the waist: others reach almost to the knee and are split front and back from hem to crutch to give freedom of movement, particularly when mounted. Some men have already broken into a run, their spears lifted above their heads as if they propose thrusting downwards at the enemy: others carry theirs at mid-thigh level, as if planning to thrust below the byrnies of the enemy. A man with an axe has already slung his shield back over his shoulders to give freedom of movement to both arms. His axe is poised to deliver the first smashing blow

67

downwards. Others have already drawn their swords and grip them with the index finger curled over the cross-guard.

As they fall on the enemy, we can see from the look in their faces and their general demeanour that they have worked themselves up into a psychological state approaching hysteria. Personal injury seems no longer to occur to them as a possibility. The axeman hurls the bright blade of his weapon downwards at the shoulder of his opponent. It is caught on the opponent's shield which shatters under the impact. The opponent retires and the axeman, swinging his weapon in figure-of-eight arcs before him, catches him with the blade at the junction of neck and shoulder with such force that his head is almost severed.

A spearman, thrusting at a groin unprotected by the byrnie, loses a hand to a sword cut. Two swordsmen have lost their shields and are using their weapons with both hands. One man has lost a leg and lies on the floor trying to protect himself from a man who stabs at him with a short sax. A man engaging a swordsman is thrust through below his byrnie by a Viking armed with a long sax.

The skirmish is over in seven or eight minutes. The enemy is either dead or fled. The Vikings pick up the weapons that lie on the ground and attend to their own dead and wounded.

The Fight in the Theatre

If we are to give credibility to the fight of this period, then there are certain clear features that we must bear in mind. There is the quality of individual action. There is the psychological feature of self-induced hypnosis that removes from a man's mind all considerations but that of victory—the 'Berserk frenzy' of the Viking. There is the uncompromising brutality, the close physical contact, the absence of any 'rules'. There is as well the high degree of physical skill in handling personal weapons, which argues a long period of training and experience. The appalling brutality of the blinding of Gloucester in *Lear* is not out of keeping with the feeling of this period, nor is the slaughter in *Macbeth* of Macduff's entire family or Malcolm's 'When I shall tread upon the tyrant's head, Or wear it on my sword . . .'

There is a further theatrical point worth remembering, particularly in connection with this period. It is not unusual to see an actor who has just vanquished an opponent, lightly toss away his sword amongst the off-stage bric-a-brac as if it meant no more to him than his cigarette-end. The most cursory glance at the literature of this period is sufficient to show that a man's personal weapons were amongst his most treasured possessions. To risk damaging his sword by casually tossing it aside, would be to risk damaging his potency as a fighter and therefore as a man. It would be no more ridiculous to see the winner of an international sports car race push his Maserati into the river before turning to receive the crowd's acclaim.

A Plot for a 'Macbeth' Fight

A fight plot for the Macbeth and Macduff encounter (Act V, sc. viii) will give an indication of how the weapons of the later part of the period might be used in the theatre.

Macbeth is fully armoured with a knee length byrnie and a conical helmet with a nasal to protect him against a blow across the face.

He carries a circular shield and a sword.

Macduff is similarly armoured. He carries a 'kite' shield and a sword. At his belt he wears a short sax in a sheath.

The tempo of the fight is slow initially, but it builds throughout in speed and violence.

SCRIPT	PHASE	MACDUFF	MACBETH
Macduff Turn hell-hound, turn!			*Turns to face Macduff.*
Macbeth Of all men else I have avoided thee. But get thee back, my soul is too much charged with blood of thine already.	*An advance of three paces.*		
Macduff I have no words		*Begins to move round Macbeth, clockwise, looking for an opening on Macbeth's right side.*	*Turns to keep Macduff in front of him. Shield held before him, sword point resting on ground.*
My voice is in my sword,		*Stops the turn. Faces Macbeth for a moment, then cries out and bursts into action. His words are like the battle-cry of a Berserk.*	*Throughout this attack, Macbeth offers no counter-attack. He has total confidence in his 'charmed life'.*

SCRIPT	PHASE	MACDUFF	MACBETH

thou bloodier
villain than terms
can give thee out!

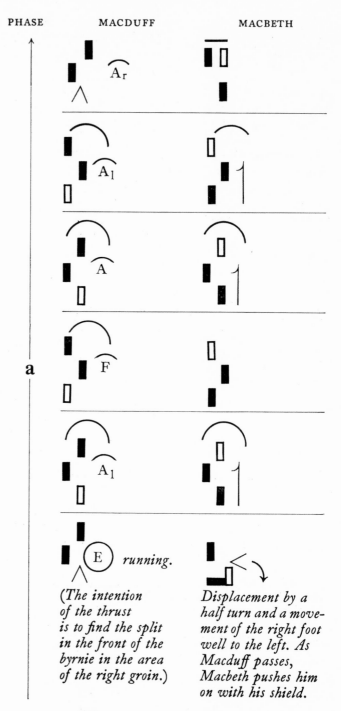

a

A_r

A_1

A

F

A_1

E running.

(*The intention
of the thrust
is to find the split
in the front of the
byrnie in the area
of the right groin.*)

*Displacement by a
half turn and a move-
ment of the right foot
well to the left. As
Macduff passes,
Macbeth pushes him
on with his shield.*

SCRIPT	PHASE	MACDUFF	MACBETH

Macduff's run carries him well past Macbeth.

Macbeth continues his turn to face Macduff again.

Macbeth Thou losest labour; as easy mayst thou the intrenchant air with they keen sword impress, as make me bleed.
Let fall thy blade on vulnerable crests; I bear a charmed life, which must not yield to one of woman born.

Macduff Despair thy charm, and let the angel whom thou still hast served tell thee, Macduff was from his mother's womb untimely ripped.

He moves back to face Macbeth again, within sword range.

b

As he says 'ripped' he appears to draw the extremity of his sword blade across Macbeth's right cheek.

Puts up his sword hand to his cheek to discover it is bleeding.

Macbeth Accursed be that tongue that tells me so, for it hath cowed my better part of man. And be these juggling fiends no more believed, that palter with us in a double sense; that keep the word of

6

SCRIPT	PHASE	MACDUFF	MACBETH
promise to our ear, and break it to our hope. I'll not fight with thee.			*Lowers his shield.*
Macduff Then yield thee coward, and live to be the show and gaze o' th' time. We'll have thee, as our rarer monsters are, painted upon a pole, and underwrit, 'Here may you see the tyrant.'		*Moves straight up to Macbeth and threatens him with the point of his sword at the unprotected level of the groin.*	
Macbeth I will not yield to kiss the ground before young Malcolm's feet, and to be baited with the rabble's curse. Though Burnham Wood be come to Dunsinane, and thou opposed, being of no woman born, yet I will try the last. Before my body I throw my warlike shield. Lay on Macduff,	**b**		*With a brisk rap of his sword he deflects the point of Macduff's weapon outside his own left thigh.*

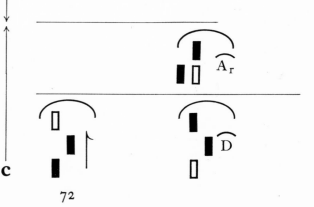

c

72

SCRIPT	PHASE	MACDUFF	MACBETH

and damned be him
that first cries
'Hold, enough!'

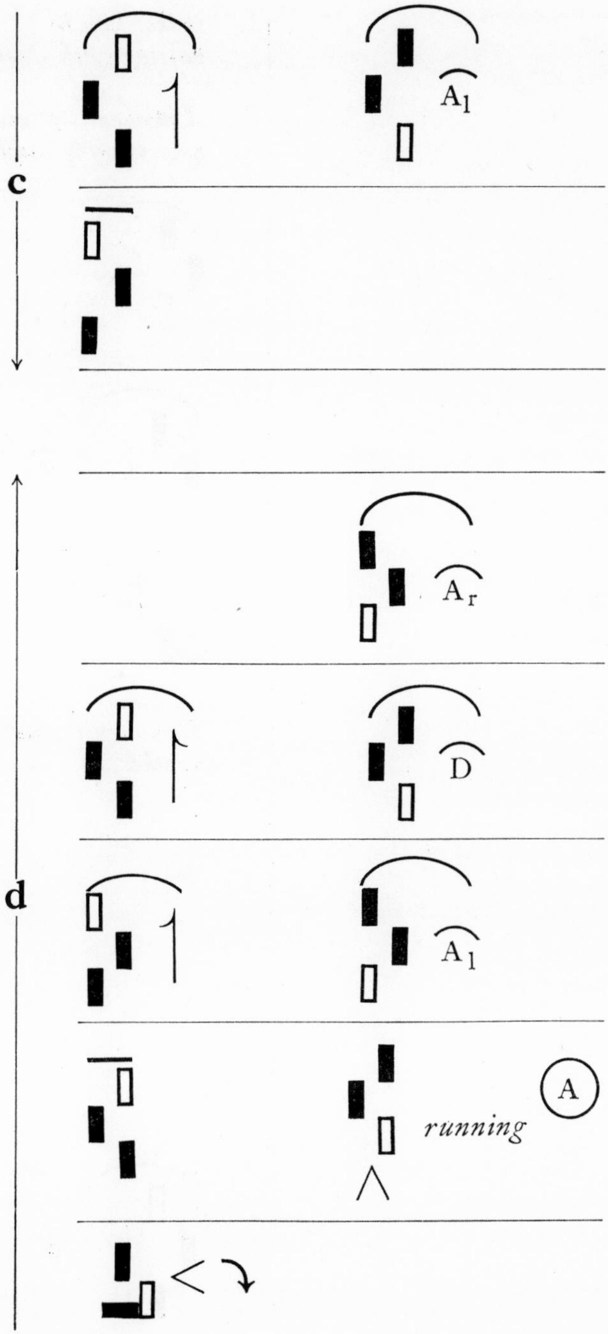

SCRIPT	PHASE	MACDUFF	MACBETH
	↓	*strikes him in passing with shield*	*Turns to face Macduff again.*

A moment's pause whilst they feel for a new opening, and then:

	e		

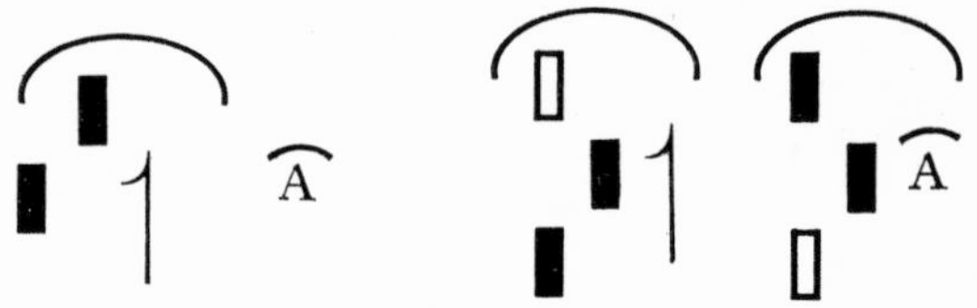

They turn through 180°, swords locked together.

	f		*Foot up to Macduff's shield. Kicks him away. Follows with an attack on the run.*

running A

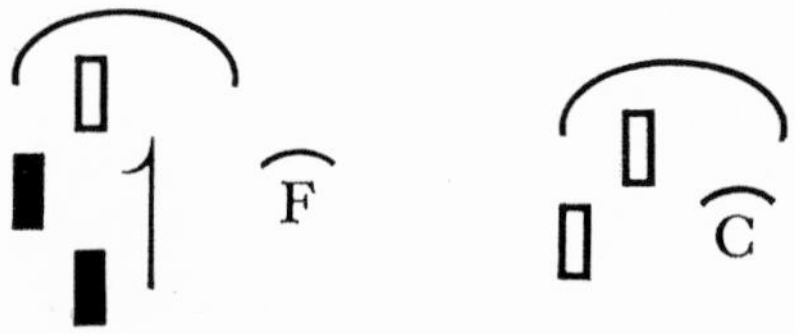

74

SCRIPT	PHASE	MACDUFF	MACBETH

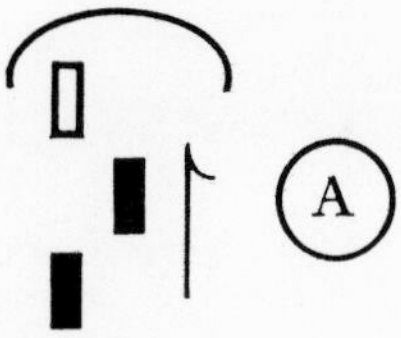

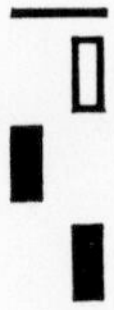

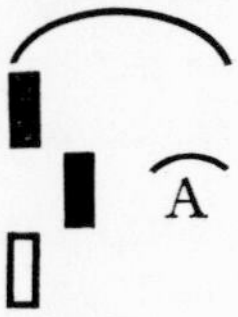

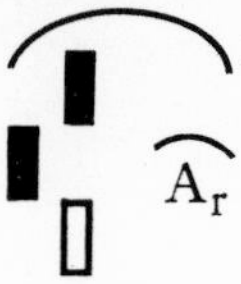

A

$\widehat{A}$

$\widehat{A}_r$

$\widehat{A}$ *(a very heavy blow)*

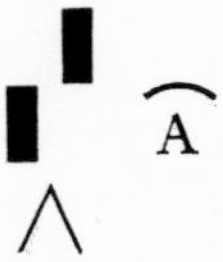

(the blow strikes the top rim of the shield and splits it open. The sword blade becomes jammed in the split. A spring-loaded split will have been previously built into the shield.)

f

Puts a foot on Macbeth's stomach and kicks him away. The shield is wrenched from Macbeth's grasp, and with it the trapped sword.

75

SCRIPT	PHASE	MACDUFF	MACBETH
			Begins to run in on Macduff.
		Throws sword and shield at Macbeth.	*Avoids the sword and shield.*
		Grasps his own shield in both hands by the edges and rushes at Macbeth.	*Force of impact knocks him to the floor. His sword falls from his grasp.*
	g	*Drops shield and leaps on Macbeth. Seizes him by throat and tries to strangle him.*	
			Throws him off at last with kicks and punches.
		Gets to his feet and draws short sax *from belt.*	*Gets to his feet. Has been injured in throat. Struggles to loosen mail at his neck.*
		Crouching low, he runs in with short sax *and stabs Macbeth upwards into the crutch.*	
Macbeth A cry as he he is struck.			
			Turns and staggers off.
		Picks up Macbeth's sword and runs after him.	

We must remember that this fight is only part of a complex battle sequence. Each part of this sequence needs to be plotted and rehearsed in detail, then all the parts need careful coordination.

76

7

Chinks in the armour: Senlac to Bosworth

Background

To generalize, we might say that the problem of the period was to find some way of cracking heavy mobile armour. One effective answer was the use of mass archers armed with the longbow, firing a barrage of 28-inch arrows over a distance up to 400 yards. Another was the use of the halberd by foot soldiers against the armoured knight on horseback.

The attitude of the authorities of the period to the professional teacher of arms is interesting. Officially it was illegal to run a school of fence. Teachers of fence, according to Aylward,[1] were 'classed as rogues and vagabonds along with players of interludes, bearwards, gipsies and other undesirable characters'. And yet the use of professional champions in the case of trial by combat, and the provision of fencing lessons for others involved in such combats, does argue the existence of a professional fencing fraternity however subterranean it might have been.

The mass attack of cavalry on halberdiers, or the barrage of arrows put up by half a thousand longbowmen, can of course be shown on film and to some extent on television. But in the theatre we are of necessity concerned with the behaviour of the individual in single combat. To understand what this behaviour must have been like and how we might adapt it to the needs of the theatre, we must first consider the range of weapons available and then look at how men equipped with different combinations of them are most likely to have fought.

The Sword
For the sake of convenience, we can distinguish three general types of sword during the period.

The Single-handed Sword
The weapon was a logical development of the sword of the Norman period. It remained a weapon capable of both cut and thrust, although a variation

---

[1] *The English Master of Arms.*

did appear towards the middle of the fourteenth century which was predominantly a thrusting weapon, no doubt designed to cope with the
plate armour that replaced mail at that time. Variations of the crossguard
were considerable and in the fifteenth century extra defences for the hand
were introduced in the form of the *pas d'âne* rings to protect the fingers, and
the large side ring to protect the knuckles. The knuckle-bow made its
appearance at the same time.

The Hand-and-a-Half Sword
In essence, the hand-and-a-half sword was a single-handed blade with a
grip long enough to be used with both hands when the occasion required.
It is more accurately associated with the later part of the period than with
the earlier. Its appearance coincides with the introduction of plate armour
in the mid-fourteenth century.

The Two-handed Sword
This was a foot weapon which made its appearance in the late fifteenth and
early sixteenth centuries. It varied in length from about 4 feet 6 inches to
6 feet. It is built as a two-handed weapon and could not have been
managed effectively with a single hand. It is questionable whether, from a
fighting point of view, it should really be regarded as a sword at all. In use
it had a good deal in common with such polearms as the pike and the
quarterstaff and it will be dealt with in more detail later.

The Dagger
The dagger, as an additional side-arm, came into wider use during this
period. Towards the end of the period it seems to have established itself
as a regular piece of equipment with both the armed man and the civilian.

The *ballock dagger* would be a typical form, particularly of the later part
of the period. It had a simple round handle of wood, with two globular
thickenings at the guard. The blade length was about 9 inches. The
misericorde was similar in general shape. Both were stabbing rather than
cutting weapons.

Polearms
The term polearm is apt. It describes accurately a weapon mounted on a
long staff. It is used here to include the quarterstaff.

The Quarterstaff   The quarterstaff was a pole of wood some 6 feet in
length, with a diameter of about 1½ inches. It was a foot weapon of both
attack and defence. In attack it could be used for both the cut and the
thrust.

The Spear During the early years of the period, the spear continued in use as a predominantly thrusting weapon. Later, it became simply one of a wide range of polearms.

The Halberd We can regard the halberd as typical of a particular range of polearms all equipped with blades on one side and spikes on the other. Many had an additional spike on top.

The halberd seems to have made its first appearance at the beginning of the fourteenth century. It was used by the foot soldier and was particularly effective against the armoured man on horseback. The rear spike could be used to pull a man off his horse; alternatively he could be struck in passing with the blade. The top spike could be used more conventionally as a spearhead. The weapon could be used at full length or at very close range, by changing the position of the hands on the pole. It was almost as manoeuvrable as the quarterstaff, and for hand-to-hand fighting was probably much superior to the modern rifle and bayonet.

We can regard such weapons as the *poleaxe* and the *bill* as falling into the same general category as the halberd for theatre purposes.

Cutting and Crushing Weapons

Many of the weapons in this group seem to have come into being in the hope that their sheer weight and the very considerable force with which they could be wielded, would provide another answer to an opponent totally encased in plate armour. Most were weapons used by fully armoured men fighting on foot.

The Axe In the early part of the period, the axe appears as a single-headed weapon usually employed with both hands. There is no question that a properly delivered blow with it, falling square on armour, would cut through it in most cases. It was essentially an attacking weapon, with scarcely any value in defence. The weapon appears less frequently in the later part of the period.

The Hammer The war hammer consisted of a heavy head of metal mounted on a staff of perhaps 4 feet in length. One side of the metal head had the characteristic shape of a hammer; the other was equipped with a spike or an axe-shaped blade. It could be used single-handed in conjunction with the shield, but in attack it must have been more effective as a two-handed weapon.

The Mace The mace, and its allies the *Morning Star* and the *Holy Water Sprinkler*, was a single-handed club. It relied on sheer weight to fracture an opponent's head or limb through armour. It was a weapon for use on foot by a man through armour. It was used in conjunction with the shield, since it had no defensive properties of its own.

79

The Ball and Chain   This is a convenient term to describe those forms of flail that consisted of a comparatively short staff with some sort of weight attached to the end by a chain or leather thongs. Like the mace, it was a single-handed weapon used mainly on foot by men in armour.

The Shield

Three types of shield are characteristic of the period.

The Triangular Shield   The long 'kite' shield of the Normans, gave way to one of triangular shape which measured some 30 inches from point to base. Many of these shields had a considerable degree of concavity, so that they tended to wrap round the side of the wearer rather like the scutum of Rome.

The triangular shield bore heraldic devices on the face. Like the 'kite' shield of the earlier period, the triangular shield is really designed for use on horseback, though there are many illustrations of its being used by men in armour on foot.

The Circular Shield   The circular shield continued throughout the period, principally for use on foot. It was a smaller weapon than that of the Viking period, having a diameter on average of some 24 inches.

The Buckler   The buckler was a much smaller circular shield that appeared with increasing frequency towards the end of the period. Its smallness made it possible for the traditional armloop to be dispensed with, so that it was held only by a handgrip placed in the centre of the back. The average diameter of the buckler was about 12 inches. It was a defensive weapon of the unarmoured man on foot.

The Bow

The Crossbow   We can distinguish two types of crossbow. The one was drawn by pulling back the string with the hands, whilst the other was so powerful that it required some mechanical attachment to cock it. Both were popular and effective weapons, particularly characteristic of the earlier part of the period. The great disadvantage of the crossbow was the comparatively long time necessary to cock it. Oakeshott[1] describes it as the 'missile weapon par excellence of the twelfth and thirteenth centuries.'

The Longbow The longbow superseded the crossbow for two reasons. In the first place it was simple and cheap to make. In the second place it had a rate of fire some five times greater than that of the crossbow. It was a weapon some 6 feet in length, stout, rather heavy, perhaps a little crude in appearance. It had a pull of up to 100 pounds and could draw a 28-inch arrow to the head. Its extreme range of effectiveness was about 400 yards.

[1] *The Archeology of Weapons.*

The Real Fight

The range of weapons and armour in this period is such that we cannot talk about a 'typical' fight. There were a number of such fights, depending on the weapons used and the personal armour of the combatants. Let us consider four fights conducted by combatants equipped with different weapons.

The Crushing Weapon

We can best see the crushing weapon in action if we imagine the fight between two men clad from head to foot in plate armour. The period is the mid-fifteenth century. The armour is not a serious encumbrance to them. It is surprisingly light and the quality of workmanship has produced such efficient articulations that the movements of each man are in no way inhibited.

Each man carries a triangular shield and wears a hand-and-a-half sword, and a dagger. One is armed with a mace, some 2 feet in length. The staff of the mace is of tubular metal, whilst the head is of forged iron. The weapon is very much head-heavy. The man's right hand passes through a leather loop attached to the end of the mace, to give him a greater security of grip. The other man carries a short flail weapon in the form of a wooden staff some 14 inches long, to the end of which is attached a heavy spiked ball of metal by a 6-inch length of chain. He, too, increases the security of his grip by passing his hand through a leather thong attached to the weapon.

The Attack and the Defence   The maceman walks at once into the attack and strikes a heavy blow obliquely at the other's head. The flailman moves his head downwards and to the left, and the mace, whose inertia is such that the direction of its movement cannot easily be changed, passes over his right shoulder. The flailman follows up his advantage by trying to trip his opponent whilst he is momentarily off-balance, but fails. He does, however, manage to catch the maceman a glancing blow on the back of his helmet with the flail. The flailman has not moved quickly enough to put any great deal of force into the blow, but it nonetheless rattles the head of the maceman and makes him stagger forward out of range.

The principal problem of the flailman is to keep the chain, with the ball on the end of it, extended. He can only do this if he makes sure that some centrifugal force is acting on the ball as he strikes. In effect, this means that he must always keep the ball in movement, describing some part of a circle. He cannot make a straight blow, but always one that meets the target at some point on the circle's circumference. For this reason his range of blows is more restricted than that of his opponent, but when he does

81

succeed in delivering a successful blow it will have more force than any struck by the mace. As the maceman turns, recovering from the jar to his head, the flailman moves into him and strikes a perfectly timed blow. The maceman meets the blow on his shield which cracks under the attack.

To prevent the successful blow being exploited, the maceman thrusts with his mace at his opponent's face and strikes him full on the visor. The shape of the visor sheds the blow, but the flailman is sufficiently dazed for a moment to be unable to follow up his advantage. The maceman thrusts at him with his shield and pushes him back by sheer weight of body, and before the flailman can recover his balance his opponent has released his grip on his own weapon so that it hangs by the leather thong from his wrist, seized the flail by the chain and dragged the weapon from his hand. He follows up his advantage with three heavy blows of the mace, all of which are taken by his opponent on the shield.

The flailman draws his sword, a formidable weapon that can be used with either one or both hands. He avoids a further blow from the mace, thrusts upwards at his opponent, and is fortunate enough to strike a point near the armpit where two plates of metal overlap. The blade enters the maceman's shoulder and puts his shield arm out of action. Since the shield is now only an encumbrance to him, he lets it slip from his arm to the floor. At the same time, he swings with the mace at the head of his opponent, who is too late to defend himself with his shield. The blow falls squarely on the side of the helmet, crushing it in towards his jaw. The flailman sinks to his knees, knocked almost unconscious. The maceman strikes him again, this time on the right shoulder, and he falls backwards. The maceman drops his mace, draws the dagger from his belt, and falls on his inert opponent. He tries with his one useful hand to lift up the visor on his opponent's helmet but it is jammed because of the blow that fell on it. But by prising with his dagger, he manages at last to move it sufficiently to strike inside with the dagger.

When the maceman gets to his feet at last and removes his helmet, his head is steaming like the flanks of a racehorse and his entire body is bathed in sweat through being encased in metal.

Bow, Sword and Buckler

A group of longbowmen stand in the gap of a hedge. They have arranged pointed stakes before them in the ground as a defence against attack by cavalry. The time is the mid-fourteenth century. Let us look closely at the activities of one of them, in the hope of understanding how he operates as a fighting man.

He wears a brimmed helmet of steel and a padded hauberk of mid-thigh length. On the inside of his left forearm is a 'bracer'—a protective strip of leather to prevent the discharging bowstring damaging the arm. He carries a single-handed broadsword at his left side together with a 12-inch buckler of wood and leather. On the right side of his waist belt he wears a dagger. Two empty quivers lie on the ground at his side and he has stuck his arrows head downwards into the earth so that he can pluck them up easily with his right hand.

The Attack and the Defence   When the enemy has closed to within 300 to 400 yards, he draws the bow, already armed with an arrow, and fires into the enemy mass. At this range he is aiming at a general body of men, rather than at one particular target. The moment his arrow has been discharged, he plucks up another with his right hand and reloads.

As the enemy closes, he begins to fire at a particular target, and later at a particular part of a target—the open vizor, for example, of an armoured man on foot. His action in firing is to pull string away from bow with both arms, much as a man today might use a spring chest expander. He leans into the bow, pushing it away from him with his left arm, pulling back on the string with his right, until the head of the arrow is drawn back almost to the woodwork of the bow, and the 'nock' fitted into the bowstring is in line with his ear. His whole bodily weight and strength seems to be put into the discharging of the arrow. An ammunition wagon keeps him supplied with arrows; if there is a substantial advance he will have an opportunity of picking up unbroken shafts from the battlefield.

Later in the battle, all his arrows discharged, he finds himself faced with a halberdier wearing a helmet and mail body armour. The archer drops his bow, draws his sword and unhooks the buckler from his belt. The halberdier cuts at his head; he avoids the blow by ducking and thrusts at the man's stomach. The thrust is not sufficiently powerful to penetrate the mail, and the halberdier strikes him on the left shoulder with a butt-stroke. The blow knocks the archer to the ground. The halberdier thrusts at him, but he rolls to one side and the point of the halberd goes into the ground.

The archer gets to his feet. His buckler is held out before him at arm's length; his sword-arm is drawn back ready to launch a counterattack against the halberdier's next attack. The halberdier, because of the length of his weapon and the weight of the mail he carries, is less manoeuvrable than the archer. Whilst the archer jigs and sways from one side to the other, trying to confuse his opponent, the halberdier has to be content with watching him and waiting for him to make a mistake. At last, thinking he has anticipated the archer's next move, the halberdier thrusts at him, increasing the length of the thrust by allowing the pole of his halberd to slide forward through his hands. The archer has planned for such an attack. He parries the blade of the advancing halberd with his buckler, and, advancing his right foot well in front of his left, steps into the halberdier with his sword and strikes him at the junction of head and left shoulder with a blow that cuts through the mail. The halberdier falls and is dispatched with the sword.

The Two-handed Sword

We can regard true two-handed sword play as beginning in the fifteenth century and running throughout the sixteenth. If we look at a meeting between two men, each armed with the weapon, in the early years of the sixteenth century, we can build an imaginative reconstruction of how they behaved.

Both men wear padded tunics with padded sleeves. Neither wears any body armour or helmet. Each carries his sword over his shoulder in the manner of a rifle, gripping the pommel or the grip with his right hand.

Each weapon approaches 6 feet in overall length. It is divided unequally into three sections. The main grip is almost $1\frac{1}{2}$ feet long and at its base is a wide but simple iron cross-guard. Some 9 inches nearer the point is another, much smaller crossguard, and the area between the two cross-guards forms a subsidiary grip. The main blade of the weapon lies between the secondary crossguard and the point.

As the two men approach one another, they lift the weapons from their shoulders and hold them with the right hand on the grip just above the main crossguard and the left hand on, or very close to, the pommel. Each extends his sword so that the point threatens his opponent. As they close to something approaching striking distance, they move round one another, at first clockwise and then anti-clockwise, trying to get the 'feel' of one another's particular fighting strengths and at the same time looking for an opening through which the first attack might be launched.

The Attack and the Defence   The attacks are made by sweeping cuts with the blade, against five main areas of the target: A; Al and B; Ar and C; D and F; E and G. We notice that the first fighter seems to manipulate the sword as if about a fulcrum set on the grip between his two hands. As one hand pushes or pulls in one direction, the other pushes or pulls in opposition, rather as the hands move on the steering wheel of a car about the central hub. At the same time, the wrists describe opposing circles with great suppleness, so that the movement of the point of the sword is extremely rapid. It describes circles and figures-of-eight. He cuts briskly at the left side of his opponent's head and, as the opponent ducks, at once reverses the direction of the blade to cut at his right thigh.

The defender relies to some extent on avoiding the attacking blade, but more frequently upon the parry. The five principal parries are those which stop the attacking blade from reaching one of the five target areas. The defender meets an attack on B, for example, by keeping his hands at the level of his waist and the point of his sword at the level of his opponent's head, and moving his blade outside the line of his left side. Similarly, he meets an attack on A by raising his weapon above his head so that it lies parallel to the ground.

Very occasionally, the attacker moves his left hand forward from the pommel on to the secondary grip, and delivers a thrust. Occasionally, too, he uses the same grip to deliver a blow at his opponent with the butt of his weapon.

The defender uses the secondary grip when he is going to parry a particularly heavy cut that might break through his ordinary grip.

Neither fighter is above using his sword or his foot to trip his opponent or otherwise disturb his balance. The fight is characterized by a good deal of fast general movement, shouts, curses and threats.

The Staff Weapon

Many staff weapons, or polearms, have uses particular to themselves, but we shall see some of the general principles of their use if we look at two combatants armed with the *quarterstaff*.

The quarterstaff that each fighter carries is some 6 feet in length and about $1\frac{1}{2}$ inches in diameter. The wood is smooth, though bruised from earlier encounters, so that the hands can slip over it with ease. The fighters are without armour or helmets. Each carries a dagger at his right hip, attached to a waistbelt.

The weapon is held rather in the manner of a rifle and bayonet, the right hand having the big knuckles on top and the left hand having the finger tips on top. The distance from the point of the weapon to the left hand is considerably more than that from the butt to the right hand. The hands are some 12 to 18 inches apart, but this distance varies considerably during the course of the fight, according to the needs of the moment. The fighters move round one another and feint a good deal before committing themselves to an attack, in the way that modern boxers feel out the strength of the opposition in the first few moments of the initial round.

The Attack and the Defence   The attacker, relying very much on the speed of his footwork, moves into his opponent very quickly and strikes a blow downwards at the crown of his head. The defender parries by raising his own weapon above his head and keeping it parallel to the ground. He follows the successful parry by sliding his right hand up the staff towards his left, stepping forward with his right foot and delivering a blow with the butt at the left side of the attacker's head. The attacker ducks to avoid the blow, slides his left hand well up the staff towards the point, and steps forward with a short thrust to the stomach. But the defender, sensing almost as he launches it that his butt stroke has been avoided, has already stepped clear of the thrust.

We can see that this sort of contest is very mobile, depending very much on the speed with which one man can sway his body out of danger, and with which the other can use his feet to carry him into and away from his opponent. We can see, too, that the weapon can be used for thrusting and that both the 'blade' and the butt can be used for cutting. The target areas being attacked are the same five as those for two-handed sword play, with which staff play has much in common. There is the area of A; that of Al and B; that of Ar and C; that of D and F; and that of E and G. It is clear from the way in which the fighters behave, that they regard head, collar-bones, arms, wrists, knees and ankles as the most vulnerable parts of the target.

Defence is by avoidance and parry. The five principal parries are designed to defend the five areas of the target, but we can subdivide these principal parries by distinguishing three different types: (a) the attacking weapon is met with the defender's blade; (b) the attacking weapon is met with the butt; (c) the attacking weapon strikes the opposing one at a point between the defender's two hands. Attacks below the waist are met with parries of type (a) and type (b). In the case of attacks above the waist, all three types of parry are possible, although in the case of attacks downwards to the crown of the head, our fighters seem almost invariably to meet them with a parry of type (c). They seem to regard the type (c) parry as being the strongest since it allows the pushing strength of both arms to be used. Parries of type (a) or type (b) require that one arm pushes whilst the other pulls, using a point on the staff between the hands as a fulcrum.

The quarterstaff is a more flexible weapon than the two-handed sword, though perhaps a good deal less lethal. The hands are much more mobile along the length of the staff, allowing the grip to be shortened or increased at will. The butt stroke is a much more regular feature of staff play than of play with the two-handed sword.

The Fight in the Theatre

The range of weapons available during this period sets very considerable problems for the actor. There is no doubt that even the flimsiest of crushing weapons that is still credible as such to an audience, can smash through a shield. The actor has a substantial problem in making the battle-axe or Morning Star look the terrifying weapon that indeed it must have been, without actually using it as such. Crudity, brute force and dogged endurance are the principal features of the fight with these weapons.

Massed archers cannot be mounted on the stage, though use could certainly be made of small numbers and of the sound of arrow flights passing overhead. In film, where massed battle scenes can be shown, actors

86

will require instruction in the disciplined use of the bow. Some adjustment to the specification of the longbow will be necessary, since it is unlikely that sufficient numbers of actors can be found to draw bows of more than a 50-pound pull and at the same time fire arrows at the rate of five or six a minute.

The sword and buckler fight will certainly be a feature of the period with a direct application to the theatre. The fight with the two-handed sword is very rarely featured on the stage, and yet it is an important form of combat of the period and has considerable theatrical possibilities. Perhaps the most spectacular fight in the theatre, could be that fought with staff weapons. The quarterstaff fight is fast, yet the weapons are large enough for an audience uninformed in arms to be able clearly to see what is going on. But it requires very careful actor training, not only in the actual use of the weapons but in timing, precision and agility. Both the quarterstaff and the two-handed sword require exercises to increase general hand mobility and control. For training and rehearsal purposes with these two weapons, masks must of course be worn and some protective padding be provided for the hands.

A Plot for a 'Richard III' Fight

Let us consider a possible plot for one fight out of the many that take place in Act V sc. iv of *Richard III*, that between Richard himself and Richmond.

Richard, fully armoured except for his helmet, completes his bellicose oration to his troops before going off to mount up.

Richard: A thousand hearts are great within my bosom:
　　Advance our standards! Set up our foes!
　　Our ancient word of courage, fair Saint George,
　　Inspire us with the spleen of fiery dragons!
　　Upon them! Victory sits upon our helms!

He goes off, followed by armourers bearing his helmet, lance, sword and shield. He is accompanied by members of his staff, also in full armour.

Act V, sc. iv: Units of *Richard's* army run in from the right and take up their positions. Halberdiers cross to the left and stand waiting to meet the first rush of cavalry. There are shouts and trumpets in the distance. The growing rumble of horsemen can be heard. Archers move in behind the halberdiers and loose two flights of arrows. A halberdier falls with an arrow in his face. The main body of halberdiers runs forward off stage with a great cry. The noise of battle offstage. The archers loose another two shafts. The halberdiers are driven back on stage in some disarray. The archers fall back; some of them break, others stand and draw swords and unhitch bucklers. Enemy swordsmen appear, together with polearm men. Shouts and trumpets. Norfolk and his supporters run in up centre, and attack the advancing enemy. Richard's archers and halberdiers rally and begin to drive back the enemy. Catesby enters up centre and fights his way to Norfolk, who lifts his visor.

SCRIPT	PHASE	RICHARD	RICHMOND

Catesby Rescue, my Lord of Norfolk! rescue, rescue! The king enacts more wonders than a man, Daring an opposite to every danger: His horse is slain, and all on foot he fights. Seeking for Richmond in the throat of death. Rescue, fair lord, or else the day is lost!

The thunder of passing cavalry. Shouts, wounded cries, trumpets. Richard appears up centre, with two or three supporters. His visor is open and his face is bleeding. He carries his triangular shield slung out of the way on his back. He grips his sword with both hands and swings it like a two-hander. There is the look of a berserk in his face.

Richard A horse!   ↑   *Cuts at halberdier.*

Richard a horse!   *Cuts at sword and buckler man.*

Richard My kingdom for a horse!   **a**   *Cuts down sword and buckler man.*

Catesby Withdraw, my lord; I'll help you to a horse.   *Fighting*

88

SCRIPT	PHASE	RICHARD	RICHMOND
Richard Slave! I have set my life upon a cast,		*Cut, cut, cut, kill*	
And I will stand the hazard of the die.		*Cut*	
I think there be six Richmonds in the field; Five have I slain today, instead of him.—A horse!	**a**	*Cut*	
a horse!		*Cut*	
my kingdom for a horse!		*He cuts his way off, followed by Norfolk, Catesby and forces.*	

Richmond and attendants enter right. Richmond lifts visor to cool off. Men run from left to right. Enter Richard, forcing before him 3 men who turn at last and run off. A cry as he sees Richmond, bearing sword and triangular shield. Richard at once moves into him, his sword point threatening the open visor.

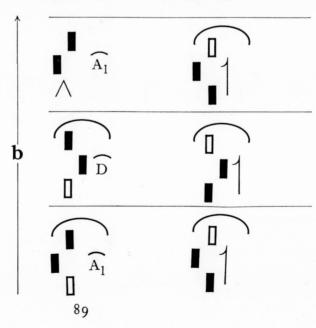

SCRIPT	PHASE	RICHARD	RICHMOND

A halberdier rushes at Richard to strike him with his blade. Richard turns through 45°, parries the staff of the halberd and cuts down the halberdier.

* The symbol, ↑, is a convenient one to indicate a parry made with both hands.

SCRIPT	PHASE	RICHARD	RICHMOND

e

A sword and buckler man rushes in and strikes Richard a disabling blow on the left forearm. His left hand falls from the pommel of his sword. He cuts single-handed at the man, who retires out of distance. Another halberdier runs in to thrust at Richard. He parries the thrust and strikes the halberdier in the face with his point. The man drops his weapon and veers away, his hands to his face.

f

Richmond's blow at D, strikes Richard on his useless left arm. A man has seized Richard's right arm at the elbow and cannot be shaken off. Richmond and his supporters crowd forward on to Richard, like dogs bating a bear. He is forced off-stage amidst the cries and clamour of battle.

This particular fight shows *Richard* in a rather romantic light. He continues to stand up under impossible odds. This interpretation stresses again the need for director and fight arranger to be absolutely clear of one another's intentions.

8

The Age of Elizabeth

Background

The age of Elizabeth was characterized by the conflict between the English broadsword and the imported rapier. The broadsword had developed into a comparatively light and manageable weapon. Although its point could be used for thrusting, it was principally a double-edged cutting weapon. It had become almost a symbol of the English fighting man.

By contrast, the rapier was an invention of Italy and Spain. It was lengthy and it was designed principally for thrusting. It was more lethal than the broadsword; however bloody a broadsword cut across the chest might be, it would probably do no more than incapacitate a man. But a thrust *through* the chest with a rapier, would almost certainly be fatal.

It became fashionable to carry and use the rapier. Italian fencing masters like Saviolo and Jeronimo settled in London, and opened schools for teaching rapier play. There was considerable opposition to the introduction of the weapon, not so much because it was a new weapon but rather because it was seen as a symbol of the growing foreign influence over English fighting styles. George Silver, a xenophobic English gentleman to the core, writes disparagingly of 'frog pricking Poiniards', and refers to the rapier as a 'Bird-spit'. Silver and his brother Toby, went so far as to challenge the Italians to public combat, with a view to demonstrating the inferiority of the rapier and the foreign style of fighting. The Italians ignored the challenge.

The Guild of Masters of Defence, the organization representing the professional teachers of fencing, held public contests as a method of examining aspirants for membership. These contests were popular, and it is unquestionable that many of the audience who saw the early Mercutios fighting the early Tybalts, were very experienced critics of sword-play. Dramatists of the period, by including fight scenes in their plays, put themselves into direct competition with the contests of the Masters of Defence, and they did so before the same audience. The fact argues a very high standard of sword-play by Elizabethan actors.

Later, the rapier and the broadsword became almost class symbols. 'Enter Sampson and Gregory with swords and bucklers of the house of Capulet', says the stage direction introducing the first act of *Romeo and*

Juliet. Sampson and Gregory, as serving-men, carry broadswords. Yet Romeo, Tybalt and Mercutio, as members of the nobility, fight with rapiers.

The Sword
The Rapier The rapier varied in overall length from about 3 feet 6 inches to almost 6 feet in a few cases. It was possible to cut with the edge of most rapiers, but the prime purpose of the weapon was for thrusting. The balance of the weapon was good.

The guard varied from an arrangement of metal rings and curved metal bands which gave good protection against a cut but little against a direct thrust at the hand, to a solid metal cup which gave full protection to the hand.

The weapon was not particularly light. In consequence, it was regarded principally as a weapon of attack. Defence was left to a dagger, a buckler, a cloak, or occasionally another rapier, held in the left hand.

The Broadsword The broadsword had an average overall length of about 3 feet 6 inches. Both edges of the blade could be used for cutting. The point could be used for thrusting where necessary. The balance of the weapon was blade-heavy, to give a greater penetration to the cut.

The guard was simpler than that of the rapier, varying from one or two simple side-rings, to side-rings, a knuckle-bow and some protection for the back of the hand. It gave good protection against the cut, but little against the thrust.

The weapon was regarded as the tool for attack. Its weight made it limited for defensive purposes. Defence was left principally to a buckler or dagger held in the left hand.

The Dagger
The dagger had a simple cross-guard and in many cases a side-ring to prevent an opponent's blade running up on to the hand. It had an average blade-length of between 12 and 18 inches. It was held, point uppermost, in the left hand, and was used almost exclusively for parrying the opponent's blade. A later dagger, the *Main Gauche*, had a curved triangle of metal sheet which gave full protection to the left hand. It was particularly suited for rapier play.

The dagger was used in conjunction with both rapier and broadsword.

The Buckler
Two forms of buckler are characteristic of the period. One had an average diameter of about 12 inches, and was gripped in the left hand by a bar that ran across the back. The other had a diameter of 18 to 24 inches. It

was held to the left forearm by a loop of leather. There was a grip for the hand.

More usually, the buckler was used in conjunction with the broadsword, but some fighters used it together with the rapier.

The Cloak

The cloak could be used defensively with either the rapier or broadsword. Held in the left hand and wrapped twice round the forearm, it provided sufficient protection to the arm to be used for parrying.

The Gloved Hand

The gloved left hand was used at times to parry a thrust from the opponent's sword. In cases of necessity, the bare left hand could be used, but the timing of the parry would need to be accurate.

Other Defensive Techniques

Almost anything that could be wielded easily, could be used in the left hand for defensive purposes. A small stool could be used effectively; so could a hat.

Polearms

Polearms were still carried in this period, but their use in the theatre is very restricted.

The Real Rapier Fight

We can only imagine what the real rapier fight must have been like, by studying the illustrations of the period, reading contemporary works, and handling the weapons ourselves. A fight between a certain Toby and a certain Andrew, for example, might have had these characteristics.

Both men are carrying rapiers in scabbards from their belts. The scabbards are in hangers. These hangers are hooked to a fixed ring on the left side of the waistbelt. The securing straps on the hangers are passed across the stomach and hooked to a sliding ring on the right side of the belt. These rings have been adjusted so that when the men turn, there is no swing of the weapons away from their bodies. Toby carries a dagger hanging from his belt in a separate scabbard. Andrew has his dagger simply thrust through his belt over his right buttock.

The men face each other, a little distance apart, and grip their scabbards with their left hands. They grip their rapiers in their right hands. Andrew has his index finger hooked round the quillon (cross-guard); Toby hooks two fingers round the quillon. Both grip the hilt as if they were gripping

94

pistols. They draw and move the points of their rapiers towards each other. Toby puts his hand down to grip his dagger, and draws it from his scabbard. Andrew puts his left hand behind his back, grips his dagger, and draws it from his belt. Both men hold their daggers as if they were very short swords; the pommel is against the heel of the hand and the thumb is on the cross-guard. Toby, who has his left hand in a heavy gauntlet, hooks his left index finger round the cross-guard. Andrew, whose hand is bare, has his four fingers curled round the grip. A blade, running up the dagger, will not injure Toby's hooked finger, because of the protection given by the gauntlet.

Neither fighter takes up a position that would be recognizable as a guard to a modern fencer. They remain out of distance of one another. They do not cross sword blades. Their positions do not guard them from any possible attack; they are rather positions from which attacks or counter attacks can be launched. Toby takes up this position:

He faces his opponent with his left foot forward. The hilt of his rapier is close to his right thigh, and he has the point directed towards his opponent's chest. His dagger is held well forward, ready to receive any possible attack.

By contrast, Andrew adopts this position:

His right foot is forward. The hilt of his rapier is at head height, his sword arm is straight, and the point of his weapon is directed towards his opponent's face. His dagger is held low, ready to parry an attack under his sword.

The Attack and the Defence   The two men begin to move round one another. They change the positions of their guards as they do so. They look a good deal more like modern wrestlers or boxers, than like modern fencers. They are looking for possible openings, and at the same time stay ready to meet any attack which the other might launch. Occasionally, one of them stamps suddenly and feints with his rapier, in the hope of trapping his opponent into making a move that will leave an opening for an attack.

The attack, when it comes, is launched with the rapier. The dagger is reserved almost exclusively for defence. Toby uses the 'pass' to get into range, as he pushes the point of his rapier forward: that is, he advances his right foot so that it passes his left. The movement carries him some five or six feet nearer to Andrew. Andrew makes use of the displacement in conjunction with his attacks; this carries him slightly to one side as his blade moves forward, so that he is out of line of any counterattack that Toby might launch.

The rapiers are used for parrying only occasionally. A thrust at the right side of the body, for example, is parried with the rapier, but most of the work of pushing aside the attacking sword-blade is left to the dagger.

The counterattack is used a good deal as a defensive move: as Andrew makes his attack, Toby immediately launches his own attack. The counter-attack is launched in such a way that it forces Andrew's sword out of line and at the same time compels him to return to the defensive.

In many cases, no parry is made at all. The attack is simply dodged by side-stepping, as a matador might step to one side to avoid the oncoming horn of a bull.

Both men are experienced fighters, so any attempt at a disarm is unlikely to be successful. Such an attempt, if it were made, would probably be made by grasping the opponent's sword by the quillons and wrenching it from his hand. Disarms by levering the sword from the opponent's hand with the dagger are possible, but they must be executed very quickly and against an opponent whose grip is insecure. Some Masters of Defence taught tripping as part of the disarm.

The Rapier Fight in the Theatre

The theatrical rapier fight must appear convincing, yet be in fact as safe as possible. It should always be exciting, and at times spectacular. Benvolio's description of the fight between Mercutio and Tybalt, quoted on page 21, shows vividly what it is necessary to aim at.

The theatrical rapier is a good deal lighter than the real thing. This is convenient for the actor who is wielding it, but it has one considerable disadvantage: it can lead to a fight that is so much faster than an authentic rapier fight, that the moves become impossible for an audience to follow. It is possible with many theatrical rapiers, for example, to do finger parries that are quite unnoticeable to a non-fencer. Such movements are theatrically useless. The moves that must be made are those which are entirely obvious to an audience. Making them obvious requires not merely a movement of the sword, but a general movement of the body, and particularly of the sword arm, that will point the movement of the actual weapons. In rehearsal, at least as much time should be given to the working out of these general movements, as to the particular movements of the sword and dagger.

There are certain characteristics of the real fight, that call for special care in the theatre. The thrust at the face, for example, was a particularly effective way of stopping an opponent, but there are less drastic ways of stopping an actor. In compensation such a move as the disarm can be made to appear highly spectacular in the theatre, when it would be too risky to attempt in a real fight.

96

The Real Broadsword Fight

Superficially, the broadsword fight had many of the features of the rapier fight. The carriage of the weapons was similar and many early writers recommended a grip with one finger round the quillon. In many cases, the fighters carried bucklers for defence, rather than daggers, but the combination of broadsword and dagger was certainly used.

As with the rapier, the guard did not actually 'guard' any part of the body. It was simply an attitude from which a fighter might more easily launch an attack. The fighters stayed out of distance, except when an actual attack was taking place. A common guard was one in which the buckler was held well out in front of the body at shoulder height, whilst the sword was held back ready to deliver a cut or a thrust, should an opening occur.

The general pattern of the fight was circular, as the fighters moved round one another. Attacks were made by moving quickly into the opponent and cutting with either edge of the blade at any exposed part of his body. Wrists and knees were favourite targets. The point of the sword was increasingly used for thrusting, during the later years of the period. Speed of footwork and precision of timing were important factors in a successful attack.

The prime defence was the buckler. It was used in the left hand to deflect or beat aside any attack. The sword, still a cumbersome affair by presentday fencing standards, was used rather for counterattacks than for parries in the modern sense. Side-stepping and moving back out of distance, were used extensively to avoid attacks rather than parrying them.

The principles governing sword and buckler play in the time of Elizabeth were crude. They tended to be more a series of tips offered by successful exponents, than the product of rational thought. The overall impression of the fight to an onlooker, must have been one of great agility and dexterity, mingled with considerable toughness.

The Broadsword Fight in the Theatre

The cut dominates the broadsword fight, as the thrust dominates the rapier fight. For this reason the broadsword fight is easier to manage in the theatre than the rapier fight. The cut demands a good deal of wrist and arm movement and the audience is therefore rarely in doubt about what is happening. The cut takes longer to make than does the thrust, so that it is difficult to speed up the fight to such an extent that its development cannot be followed by the audience.

But whereas it is possible to thrust a little off the body on occasions, in the rapier fight, it is essential that cuts with the broadsword be aimed *at*

97

the body. Whatever the actors themselves might feel, cuts aimed at the buckler or at the opponent's sword, are immediately apparent as such to an audience. The attitude, 'You hit my sword, then I'll hit yours', immediately robs the fight of any authenticity for the audience. A sounder attitude would be, 'I'm going to hit you, and heaven help you if you don't stop me'.

What it is necessary for the actor to fake, is the force of the cut. In the real fight, the cut would be delivered with as much force as possible. In the theatre this force must only be apparent.

Movement, speed and agility should characterize the fight. Such movement requires as much rehearsal as a dance routine.

A Plot for the 'Hamlet' Fight

Hamlet and Laertes face one another. Both carry a rapier and a dagger.

SCRIPT	PHASE	HAMLET	LAERTES
Hamlet Come on, sir.			
Laertes Come, my lord. (*They play.*)		*They move round one another through 180°, trying out different guards to test the other's reaction.*	

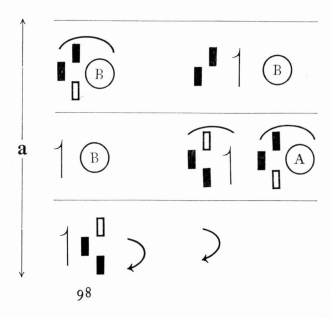

SCRIPT	PHASE	HAMLET	LAERTES

They turn through 180° *with their swords locked and their bodies* corps à corps. *Each tries to push the other away. At last they break and drop into new guards.*

* The *corps à corps* position is one in which the fighters are so close to one another that their bodies are touching.

99

SCRIPT   PHASE   HAMLET   LAERTES

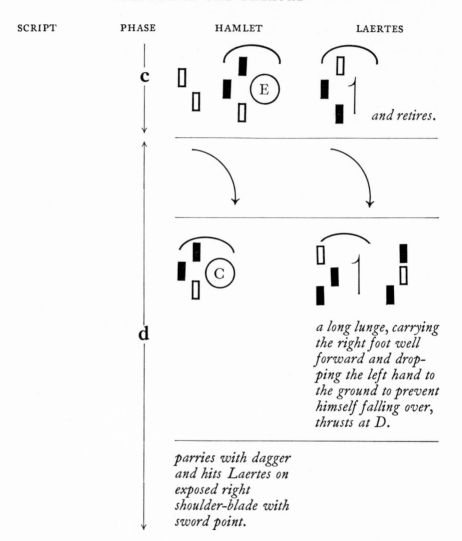

c

and retires.

d

*a long lunge, carrying
the right foot well
forward and drop-
ping the left hand to
the ground to prevent
himself falling over,
thrusts at D.*

*parries with dagger
and hits Laertes on
exposed right
shoulder-blade with
sword point.*

Hamlet One.

Laertes No.

Hamlet Judgement.

Osric A hit, a very
palpable hit.

Laertes Well; again.

SCRIPT	PHASE	HAMLET	LAERTES

King Stay; give me drink. Hamlet, this pearl is thine; Here's to thy health.
(*Trumpets sound, and cannon shot off within.*) Give him the cup.

Hamlet I'll play this bout first; set it by awhile. Come.
(*They play.*)

They repeat phase **a**, *then:*

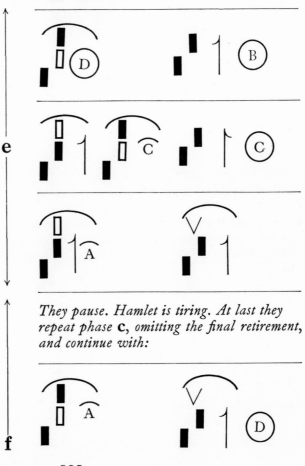

e

They pause. Hamlet is tiring. At last they repeat phase **c**, *omitting the final retirement, and continue with:*

f

SCRIPT	PHASE	HAMLET	LAERTES

*and an
advance*
to corps à corps

*Breaks by retirement
and cuts C.*

f

*then a long
lunge
accompanied
by displacement to
the left, hitting
Laertes at C under
his sword arm, with
the point.*

Hamlet Another hit;
what say you?

Laertes A touch, a
touch, I do confess.

King Our son shall
win.

Queen He's fat, and
scant of breath.
Here Hamlet, take my
napkin, rub thy brows:
The queen carouses
to thy fortune,
Hamlet.

Hamlet Good madam!

King Gertrude, do
not drink.

Queen I will, my lord;
I pray you, pardon me.

King (aside): It is the
poison' cup: it is too
late.

SCRIPT	PHASE	HAMLET	LAERTES

Hamlet I dare not
drink yet, madam; by
and by.

Queen Come, let me
wipe thy face.

Laertes My lord, I'll
hit him now.

King I do not think't.

Laertes And yet it is
almost against my
conscience.

Hamlet Come, for the
third, Laertes; you but
dally; I pray you,
pass with your best
violence; I am afeared
you make a wanton of
me.

Laertes Say you so?
come on. (*They play.*)

They repeat phase e *at increased speed.
There is a momentary pause, then:*

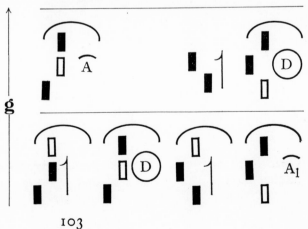

SCRIPT	PHASE	HAMLET	LAERTES

ĝ

*steps
corps à
corps,
so that both swords
and daggers are
locked together.
Makes an attempt
to trip Laertes,
but fails.*

*They turn through 180°. Finally, they
succeed in pushing one another away. They
repeat phase ĝ, excluding the 180° turn.
Laertes' push away is much more violent on
this repeat.*

h

*stabs with dagger
at C.*

They break.

Osric Nothing,
neither way.

*Lowers weapons
and begins to
step away.*

SCRIPT	PHASE	HAMLET	LAERTES
Laertes Have at you now!	↑ i ↓	*Laertes steps forward quickly and stabs Hamlet in the left arm with the poisoned weapon. Hamlet drops his dagger. He realizes that Laertes' weapon is not 'foiled'. Laertes can see that Hamlet is wounded, and yet he clearly intends to continue the fight. Hamlet begins to grasp the truth of the situation. He rushes at Laertes and disarms him by seizing the poisoned weapon by the quillons and wrenching it out of his grasp. In the process he drops his own rapier. Laertes is left with a dagger. As Hamlet advances on him, he picks up Hamlet's rapier from the floor. Hamlet makes a sudden movement with his left arm that distracts Laertes's attention for a moment. Hamlet appears to stab Laertes, by passing the poisoned rapier under the armpit away from the audience.*	
King Part them; they are incensed.			
Hamlet Nay, come, again. (*The Queen falls.*)			

A Plot for a 'Romeo and Juliet' Fight

As an example of a fight between two sword and buckler men of the period, let us look at that between *Sampson* and *Abraham* in Act I, sc. i.

Sampson has had his courage doubted by Gregory, a few minutes earlier. Let us assume that in the opening phase of the fight, he is out to refute his colleague's suggestion.

Both the fighters are armed with broadswords and hand-bucklers.

SCRIPT	PHASE	SAMPSON	ABRAHAM
Sampson Draw if you be men; Gregory, remember thy washing blow. (*They fight.*)	↑ a	*Rushes at once into the attack*	

SCRIPT	PHASE	SAMPSON	ABRAHAM

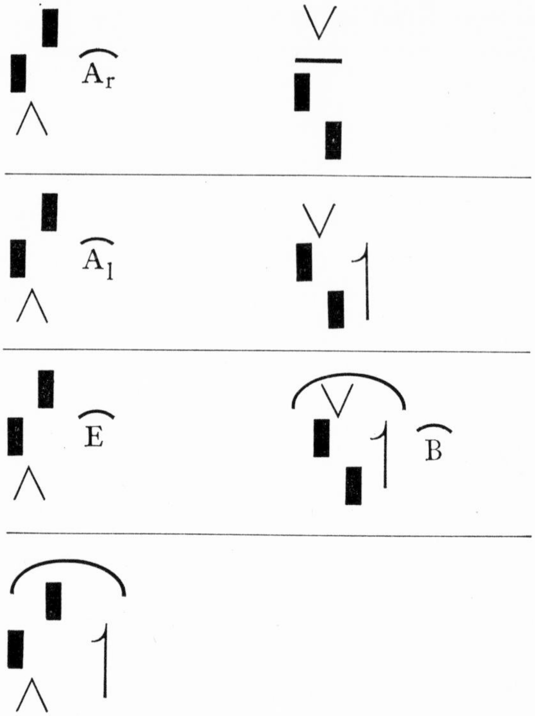

and advances to
corps à corps. *Puts
foot up to Abraham's
stomach and pushes
him away.*

*They turn through 90°. Abraham is
constantly changing his guard as he expects
the next attack to come first from below and
then from above. Sampson repeats phase* **a**,
as far as the corps à corps *position, then
Benvolio rushes between them and tries to
drag them apart.*

Benvolio Part fools.
Put up your swords,
you know not what you
do. (*Enter Tybalt.*)

SCRIPT	PHASE	SAMPSON	ABRAHAM

Tybalt What art thou drawn among these hartless hinds? Turn thee Benvolio, look upon thy death.

Benvolio I do but keep the peace, put up thy sword, Or manage it to part these men with me.

Tybalt What drawn and talk of peace? I hate the word as I hate hell, all Montagues and thee: Have at thee coward. (*They fight.*)

c

Abraham has been pushed away by Benvolio. When Sampson turns, he finds himself facing Abraham's friend who is even less cautious than Sampson has been.

The friend rushes to the attack and repeats phase **a**, *making the moves previously made by Sampson. Sampson is forced to make the moves previously made by Abraham. From the* corps à corps *position in phase* **a**, *they continue:*

Pushes Sampson away, then:

SCRIPT	PHASE	SAMPSON	FRIEND

A_1

G

d

A

E

then runs up sword blade until hilts lock.

(Enter three or four Citizens with clubs or partisans.)

Officer Clubs, bills and partisans, strike, beat them down, Down with the Capulets, down with the Montagues.

9

The Age of Transition:
the Seventeenth Century

Background

The age was one of transition for the swordsman in two ways. In the first place, the rapier itself was moving from the weapon of the Elizabethan age towards the small sword of the eighteenth century. In the second place, a system of sword play was developing that finally put the activity on a scientific basis, the same basis in fact that we recognize in modern sword play.

Early in the period, with the Masters of Defence firmly and openly established, the teaching of fencing was accepted if still not entirely approved. Fencing was regarded as part of the education of a gentleman, designed still to fit him to defend himself in the event of attack, rather than as a sportive activity.

But the authority and prestige of the gild of Masters waned later in the period. Their prize fights, which had been serious examinations of a man's fitness to teach fencing, were replaced in popularity by the spectacles of the gladiators. The gladiators were professional fighters who gave demonstrations of arms in public as a form of rather bloody entertainment. In conjunction with this activity, they gave lessons in the use of arms.

During the period, a body of literature on the use of arms—in particular the use of the sword—was built up. Some of this literature was English: much was French and Italian. In a sense, the heyday of personal combat was disappearing as the practice of the sword moved into more esoteric realms. More theorizing necessarily meant that the pupil had more to learn. Few men of affairs could have found the increasing amount of time necessary to master quite complex systems of the use of the sword. And indeed, many men must have worn a sword during the later part of the period for no better reason than that it was still regarded as part of the dress of a gentleman.

The Sword
The Transition Rapier   The Elizabethan battle for supremacy between the imported rapier and the English broadsword was won in the early seven-

teenth century by the rapier. The broadsword was still in use, but it was no longer the principal weapon of personal combat.

The triumph of the rapier over the broadsword, was the triumph of the thrust over the cut. Once this had been established, the rapier developed in such a way that it became increasingly efficient as a thrusting weapon and relied less and less upon the use of the edge. The blade became narrower, since it no longer needed to carry a substantial cutting edge. This narrowing produced a weapon considerably lighter than its precursor, and this lightening produced a range of other possibilities. It meant that the weapon was much faster in use, and could in consequence be used not only for attack but also for defence. Since the left hand was no longer of paramount importance for defence, a different guard position could be adopted so that less of the target was presented to the opponent. Increased lightness meant increased mobility and increased mobility meant that the considerable blade length of many Elizabethan rapiers was no longer necessary. Above all, the development of the transition rapier meant that a formalized system of fencing based on rational principles could be established.

A typical transition rapier might still be capable of delivering a cut. It would have a blade narrower and shorter than the Elizabethan rapier. It would have a simplified guard of a dish or shell shape, the vestiges of a cross-guard and perhaps a simple knuckle-bow.

The Broadsword

The broadsword, though still in use in various forms, gradually lost its position as a serious rival to the rapier. It continued to be used for practice purposes, and was one of the weapons with which the gladiators gave their exhibitions.

The Dagger

As the rapier became light enough to handle defence as well as attack, the dagger began to disappear from use. A typical later form is the *Main Gauche*, with its guard of triangular sheet metal giving considerable protection to the hand.

The Buckler

The buckler fell into almost complete disuse during this period, though it was still to be seen in gladiatorial combats for some years to come.

The Left Hand

The use of the left hand in defence began to be discouraged by the leading teachers. Nonetheless, it was some considerable time before the left hand, usually protected by the gauntlet, ceased to be used at all in defence.

The Real Seventeenth-century Rapier Fight

Films made on the theme of Dumas's *Three Musketeers* give the impression of fighting in this period as having totally outgrown the crudities of earlier days. Yet contemporary fencing literature and illustrations confound this view. The trip was still regarded as a legitimate move, and serious combatants with their lives at stake could hardly have disdained the use of any device that would give them an advantage over an opponent.

Let us reconstruct a hypothetical duel between a certain Lord Andrews and a Mr Benn, which takes place in Lincoln's Inn Fields about the middle of the century. Both gentlemen are stripped to their shirts. Both carry rapiers with a blade length of about 33 inches. Each weapon has a circular, dished guard, a simple, short cross-guard and a knuckle-bow. Each man wears a leather gauntlet on his left hand. They come on guard out of distance: that is, neither can hit the other by simply extending his sword arm. Both men adopt the same guard, a guard quite different from any of the rather loose positions of Elizabethan rapier play. To begin with, they no longer stand square on to one another. They stand sideways, exposing only their right sides. Their feet are some 24 inches apart, left knees are bent and right knees straight. Sword arms are partly extended, points of the weapons threatening chests. The sword hand is on a level with the waist; the elbow of the sword arm is slightly bent. The left hand of each man is held in line with the head, and on a level with the left eye, ready to be used occasionally in defence, or in the case of a disarm by seizure of the opposing weapon.

The Attack and the Defence   Andrews shoots his arm forward. Benn automatically reacts by moving his weapon to parry, but Andrews's move is a feint to test the speed of his opponent's reactions. Andrews feints again at the face and Benn retires a pace by stepping backwards first with his left foot and then with his right. In this initial period of skirmishing, we notice that the fighters no longer move round one another, as they did in earlier periods. Their movements are back and forward along an imaginary straight line.

Benn launches the first serious attack with a pass to carry him into distance, followed by a lunge. That is, he moves his left foot forward so that it passes his right, and then, as he straightens his sword arm and directs the point at his opponent's chest, he advances his right foot some 24 inches, bending the knee, and straightens his left leg. As he moves forward, he drops his left hand to the ground, to prevent himself from falling over. The move is a rash one. Andrews, anticipating it, steps to his right to avoid Benn's point, and stabs him through the fleshy part of the upper left arm. Benn immediately returns to the guard position. For some time, both fighters are careful not to overreach themselves.

Benn, now troubled by the wound in his left arm, makes a determined effort to finish off his opponent quickly. He advances with a pass and feints at B. As Andrews parries, Benn *deceives* the parry by dipping the point of his sword below his opponent's blade, and lifting it again on the other side, and lunges to hit Andrews high at C. The wound is painful and inconvenient, but not fatal. Andrews retires at once, taking care to threaten Benn still with the point of his sword, in case Benn decides to follow up the opening. Benn advances, carrying his right foot forward first, then following it with his left, and lunges at D. Andrews retires and parries. Again Benn advances and lunges at B. Andrews retires, parries the lunge and cuts down at Benn's wrist. Benn manages to draw back his weapon sufficiently to take the blow on his blade.

Andrews feints at A, to break Benn's developing aggression. Benn retires. There are more feints and abortive parries. Benn suddenly stamps on the ground and gives a sudden shout, in an attempt to increase the tension in Andrews. Then he advances and lunges at D. Andrews parries the thrust with his left hand, steps forward and threatens Benn at the throat with the point of his sword. Benn hesitates a moment, then drops his weapon and acknowledges defeat.

The Seventeenth-century Rapier Fight in the Theatre

The comparative lightness of the seventeenth-century rapier, means that the fight in the theatre can increase in speed and in spectacular quality. But this brings additional difficulties. If the fight is faster, then the fight plot must stress the need for those general movements which will point the movement of a blade, since that blade might move too quickly for an audience to follow its progress. If there is to be a development in spectacle, then the physical demands on the actors will be increased. Some actors, indeed, will not be physically equipped to meet great increases in agility.

Again, the nature of seventeenth-century rapier play depended on a knowledge of the developing system of fencing. It required a systematic dexterity in handling the weapon for both attack and defence. An actor who is to succeed in such a fight will need a background of at least the basic moves of modern épée play.

The comparative lightness of the weapon, which in the real fight was its principal virtue, adds considerably to the danger of using it in the theatre. Even when thoroughly flattened at the point and robbed of its edges, as any theatrical weapon must be, it can still blind an actor who is not thoroughly prepared to receive a particular move. Only the most detailed plotting of the fight beforehand, followed by the most rigorous rehearsal, can ensure the safety of the actors. The ability to *ad lib*, to cover up a forgotten line of dialogue, might be regarded as a virtue in an actor. But the need to engage in unrehearsed *free play* to cover a forgotten *move*, can very easily lead to disaster.

A Plot for a 'Cyrano' Fight

The fight, between *Cyrano de Bergerac* and the *Viscount de Valvert*, is from Act I sc. iv.

SCRIPT	PHASE	CYRANO	VISCOUNT
Cyrano (calling out as if he had been seized with the cramp): Aie! Aie!			
Viscount (who was going away, turns back): What on earth is the fellow saying now?			
Cyrano (with grimaces of pain): It must be moved, it's getting stiff, I vow—This comes of leaving it in idleness! Aie! . . .			
Viscount What ails you?			
Cyrano The cramp! cramp in my sword!			
Viscount (drawing his sword): Good!			
Cyrano You shall feel a charming little stroke!			
Viscount (contemptuously): Poet! . . .			
Cyrano Ay, poet, Sir! In proof of which			

SCRIPT   PHASE   CYRANO   VISCOUNT

while we fence, presto!
all extempore I will
compose a ballade.

Viscount A ballade?

Cyrano Belike you know
not what a ballade is.

Viscount But . . .

Cyrano (*reciting as
if repeating a lesson*):
Know then that the
ballade should contain
Three eight-versed
couplets . . .

Viscount (*stamping*): Oh!

Cyrano (*still reciting*):
And an *envoi* Of four
lines . . .

Viscount You . . .

Cyrano I'll make one
while we fight, And
touch you at the final
line.

Viscount No!

Cyrano No?
(*declaiming*) The duel
in Hotel of Burgundy
—fought By De
Bergerac and a good-
for-nought!

Viscount What may
that be, and if you
please?

Cyrano The title.

The House (*in great
excitement*): Give room!

114

SCRIPT	PHASE	CYRANO	VISCOUNT

—Good sport!—Make place.—Fair play!— No noise! (*Tableau. A circle of curious spectators in the pit; the* Marquises *and* Officers *mingled with the common people; the* Pages *climbing on each other's shoulders to see better. All the women standing up in the boxes. To the right,* De Guiche *and his retinue. Left,* Le Bret, Ragueneau, Cyrano, *etc.*)

Cyrano (*shutting his eyes for a second*): Wait while I choose my rhymes . . . I have them now! (*He suits the action to each word.*)

I gaily doff my beaver low, And, freeing hand and heel, My heavy mantle off I throw,

Walks away from Viscount, removing various garments and handing them to supporters.

And I draw my polished steel.

Draws. Makes three or four rapid cuts in the air, and a number of brisk circular parries.

Graceful as Phoebus, round I wheel, Alert as Scaramouch, A word in your ear, Sir Spark, I steal—At the *envoi's* end, I touch! (*They engage.*)

Turns to face Viscount.

115

SCRIPT   PHASE   CYRANO   VISCOUNT

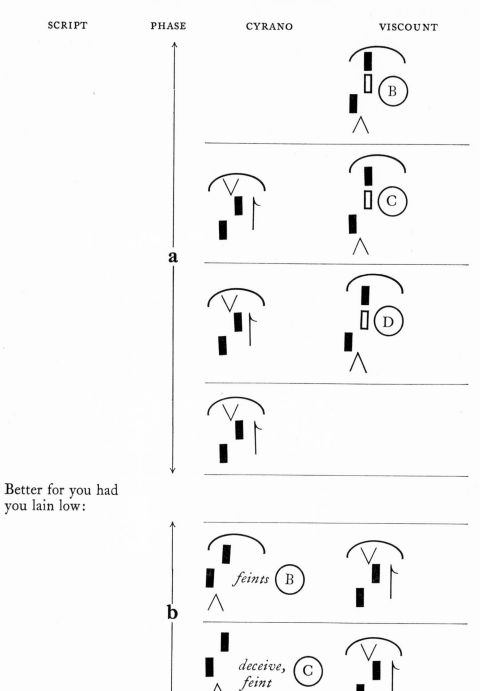

Better for you had
you lain low:

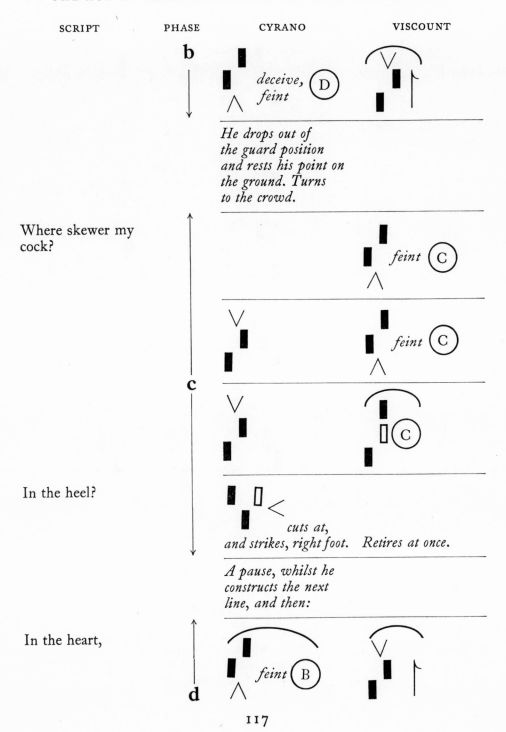

SCRIPT   PHASE   CYRANO   VISCOUNT

deceive, feint

He drops out of the guard position and rests his point on the ground. Turns to the crowd.

Where skewer my cock?

feint

feint

In the heel?

cuts at, and strikes, right foot.   *Retires at once.*

A pause, whilst he constructs the next line, and then:

In the heart,

feint

SCRIPT	PHASE	CYRANO	VISCOUNT

your ribbon blue
below?

deceive and cut through ribbon with point of sword.

In the hip, and make
you kneel?

he strikes him on hip   Retires

Ho for the music of
clashing steel;

circular,

deceive
and strikes him in
upper right arm.

—What now?—A
hit?

Steps up to Viscount and makes elaborate play of examining the wound.

d

SCRIPT	PHASE	CYRANO	VISCOUNT

Not much! 'Twill be
in the paunch the
stroke I steal, When
at the *envoi*, I touch.

*Gives Viscount an
affectionate tap on
stomach.*

Oh for a rhyme, a
rhyme in o?—

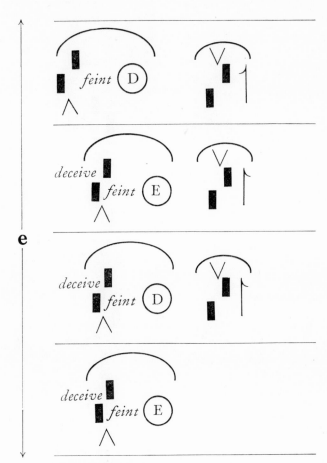

e

You wriggle, starch-
white, my eel?

A rhyme! a rhyme!

*Puts out his left
hand, as if to hold
up his opponent
whilst he composes
the rhyme in 'o'.
At last he has it.*

SCRIPT	PHASE	CYRANO	VISCOUNT

the white feather you
show!

*The remark goads
Viscount into a last
frenzy of action.*

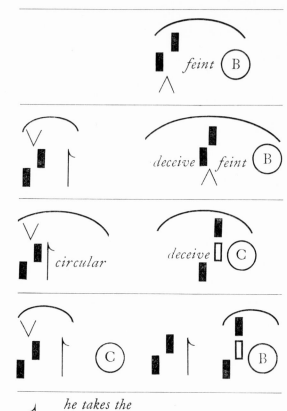

Tac! I parry the point
of your steel;

*he takes the
Viscount's
blade between
thumb and two
fingers, and removes
it from the target as
if it were a bit of
fluff that he had
plucked off his
clothes.*

—The point you hoped
to make me feel;

SCRIPT	PHASE	CYRANO	VISCOUNT
I open the line, now clutch your spit, Sir Scullion—show your zeal!		*Throws both arms wide and stands square to Viscount, his whole target exposed.*	E
At the *envoi's* end,	ġ		
I touch!		*Draws the point of his sword backwards across the Viscount's chest, ripping his clothing.*	
(*He declaims solemnly.*) *Envoi.*		*Steps back out of distance.*	
Prince, pray Heaven for your soul's weal!		*Comes on guard again. This time he clearly is in earnest.*	*On guard.*
I move a pace—	h		
lo, such!		*feint* B	*circular*
		deceive, feint B	

SCRIPT	PHASE	CYRANO	VISCOUNT

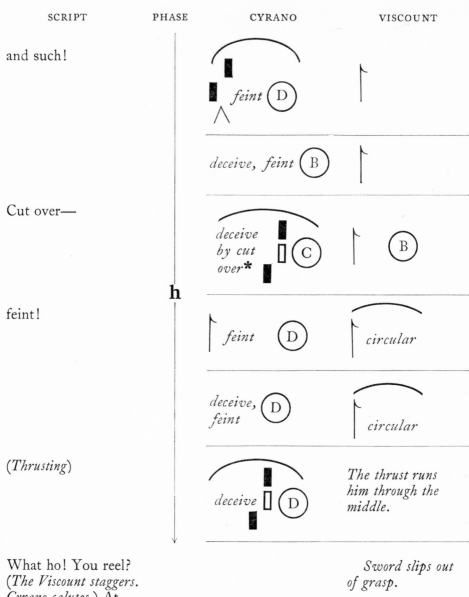

and such!

Cut over—

feint!

(*Thrusting*)

What ho! You reel?
(*The Viscount staggers.
Cyrano salutes.*) At
the *envoi's* end, I
touch!

*Sword slips out
of grasp.*

* The *cut over* is a technique for deceiving a parry by lifting the blade up and over the top of the opponent's point, and bringing it down again on the other side of his blade. It is a technique of modern fencing which is probably an anachronism here. The author clearly has modern épée or foil fencing in mind, rather than authentic seventeenth-century rapier play.

10

Style & Expediency: The Eighteenth Century

Background

The late seventeenth century saw the arrival of the small sword, a weapon which was to dominate the scene of personal defence, until combat with the sword finally disappeared. But, although it was the principal personal weapon of the eighteenth century, it was still not the only one. Cutting weapons continued to develop and to be used both in practice and in serious combat.

The professional gladiators, who continued to give their gory displays until the middle of the period, kept in use a wide range of otherwise out-moded weapons, many of which had their origins in the medieval period. These were the days of the great James Figg, who fought more than 270 professional battles, and claimed to have been defeated only once. One element of eighteenth-century sword play arises from such practitioners as these, and from such experienced soldiers as Donald McBane.

The second element of sword play in the period, is represented by the growth of the fencing theorists, who had not necessarily ever used the sword in serious combat. This second element, represented in Britain by such men as Sir William Hope, produced a fixed style of fencing, with a system of proscriptions not necessarily of value in combat. The target was defined as excluding the head, arms and legs, for example, and hits which in practice landed off the target were frowned on, despite their possible value in combat. Use of the left hand was permissible only under the most unusual circumstances. Intentional thrusts at the face, disarming and tripping, were, on the whole, severely discouraged. The displacement, although taught by many Masters, was not regarded as a serious defensive move. In essence, all attack and defence had to be carried out with the blade alone. The circular, or counter-parry, was beginning to be acceptable, though even at the end of the period the simple parries of what we would now call *quarte*, *tierce* and *seconde* predominated.

The teaching of fencing, although still principally designed to equip a pupil to defend himself against serious attack, was already beginning to be regarded as the teaching of a gentlemanly accomplishment in its own right. Stress was laid on the need, in serious combat, to keep the moves as simple as possible.

Fencing literature grew in volume during the period, much of it with its origins in France.

The Sword

Small Sword   This was exclusively a thrusting weapon. As such, it was entirely lethal. The average blade length was about 33 inches. The hand was protected by a metal guard in the shape of a double shell. The old cross-guard of the rapier had quite disappeared, and protection for the back of the hand was in the form of a simple knuckle-bow. Since the small sword was an essential feature of the dress of a gentleman, though he might never draw it in anger in his life, many swords of the period are lavishly decorated with precious metals, enamels and jewellery.

The weapon was used for both attack and defence.

Cutting Sword   The cutting sword was certainly still in use. The gladiators used it, and it was used to some extent in the duel. The *back-sword* was a single-edged weapon, and practice with it formed part of a total fencing education. The *falchion* was a short and rather heavy weapon, with a slight curve to the blade. It was closely related to the *cutlass*, the *dusack* and the *hanger*. The *spadroon* was a lighter weapon, capable of both cut and thrust. It seems to have been a rather unsatisfactory compromise between the two methods of use.

Other Methods of Attack and Defence

Despite the demand by the purists for 'correctness' of style and usage, the writings of the practitioners of the period mention methods of defence and attack more in keeping with the facts of life. Attacks preceded by a handful of sand in the face are mentioned. A hat could be thrown at an opponent's face; so could a sword or a cloak. The hat could be used in defence by offering some protection to the left hand. It could also be used to conceal a small pistol. The cloak could be thrown over the opponent's sword, putting it momentarily out of action. It could also be used in defence, either loose or wrapped a couple of turns round the left forearm. The jacket would serve a similar purpose.

Gentlemen were warned about the possibility of attack in narrow alley-ways. They were warned, too, about the attack at night with lantern and dagger, where the technique was to dazzle a man by thrusting a lighted lantern in his face, and then skewer him with the dagger.

124

The Real Small Sword Fight

It might be of interest theatrically, to imagine a meeting between devotees of the two views of fencing with the small sword. John Howard has been educated in fencing according to the views of Hope and his successors. He uses only his blade for both attack and defence, eschewing such vulgarities as the disarm, the use of the left hand and the displacement. He comes on guard with his sword arm slightly bent at the elbow, his hand on a level with his waist, and the point of his weapon threatening the lower chest of his opponent. He holds his sword with all four fingers on the grip. His feet are some 24 inches apart, the left knee bent and the right straight. Only the right side of his body is presented to his opponent, and his carriage is upright. If anything, he leans a little backward, as if to keep his face out of reach of his opponent's point. His left arm is raised in an arc behind him, the hand on a level with the top of his head and a good 10 inches behind it.

By contrast, the style of George Blake indicates an education from a Master who puts expediency before rules. His guard position differs considerably from that of his opponent. His feet are some 18 inches apart, and, although they are placed one behind the other with the right leading, his body position is much squarer than Howard's. In his left hand he holds his empty scabbard about the central point, and has it ready at the level of his left breast to use in much the same way as a dagger in the old rapier and dagger play. His sword arm is extended, the elbow a little bent and the point threatening his opponent's midriff. He holds his weapon more by the pommel than by the grip, and in consequence has a reach of 2 or 3 inches more than Howard.

The Attack and the Defence

Blake begins at once to harass his opponent by beating his blade with the blade of his own weapon. Howard finds this particularly irritating. He has not been schooled in this kind of behaviour, and whenever he receives a beat and threatens Blake with his point, Blake at once retires out of distance, only to return again a second later.

Blake, having satisfied himself about the kind of opponent he is facing, decides to launch a serious attack on Howard's face. He does this by extending his sword arm fully and feinting at B. As Howard moves his sword to his left to defend himself with a simple parry, Blake deceives the parry by dipping his point below it, raises the point to threaten Howard's face, and gives a half lunge by advancing his right foot some 6 inches, bending his right knee and straightening his left. Howard instinctively retires and parries. He is fortunate enough to catch Blake's blade and deflect it from the target. But it is quite clear now to Blake that Howard regards attacks

125

on the face as being in breach of the code of fencing rules by which he operates. Blake capitalizes this in the next phase of the engagement, by attacking Howard's sword hand and forearm, a form of attack most disturbing to Howard.

Howard launches his first serious attack by a feint at D, which Blake meets with a parry. Howard deceives the parry and feints at E. Again Blake parries and again Howard deceives the parry. With a full lunge—his feet are some 40 inches apart—he thrusts at B. Blake parries successfully with his scabbard as if it were a dagger. Howard is now too close to him for Blake to be able to bring the point of his sword into play immediately. He satisfies himself with a solid whack to the right side of Howard's head with his scabbard. Howard recovers from the parry and retires at once out of distance.

Howard is now much clearer about the nature of Blake as a swordsman. Although he is not practised in dealing with such a man, at least he is much more wary of him. He decides that under no circumstances must he take his eyes off him or allow himself to be distracted for a moment. When Blake warns him about another attacker who, he claims, is about to fall on Howard from behind, Howard ignores the warning and continues to watch Blake's every movement. His only hope is to put full confidence in the style of fencing that he has been taught, in the belief that it is intrinsically superior to the expediencies of Blake.

Blake drops the point of his scabbard to the ground, whilst keeping Howard's attention on the movements of his point which are again threatening Howard's sword arm. Then, with a flick of his left wrist, Blake tries to toss a little dust into Howard's eyes with the scabbard point. But Howard, having seen the move out of the corner of an eye, retires at once, and parries the thrust that Blake launches in conjunction with the dust attack. Blake has placed a little too much faith in the trick, and when Howard, having parried the opposing blade, replies at once with a counter-thrust, Blake is hit through the left arm and the scabbard drops from his fingers.

Howard advances to follow up the opening he has created and finish off his opponent, but he is met by Blake's *round parade*. This is a form of general *counter-parry* executed with an extended sword arm and a continuous circular movement of the point in a clockwise direction. Blake, now losing a considerable amount of blood from the wound in his left arm, realizes that he must finish the fight as soon as possible. He beats Howard's blade aside and steps towards him with the intention of either seizing his blade and wrenching it from his hand, or tripping him and at once dispatching him on the ground. But as he steps forward, Howard again retires, feints B, C, B, deceives a further parry from Blake, and lunges to hit him in E. Blake falls.

126

Although in this particular encounter we see the triumph of Howard's style of fighting, we would be rash to conclude that such a style was necessarily superior on all occasions to that employed by Blake.

The Small Sword Fight in the Theatre

The small sword of the eighteenth century is perhaps the most lethal non-percussion weapon ever developed. This presents a particular problem in the theatre, since whatever precautions are taken in the manufacture of a theatrical reproduction, that reproduction must necessarily retain many of the lethal features of the original. Detailed planning of the fight and meticulous rehearsal are essential if the safety of the actors is to be guaranteed. Thrusts at the face should be avoided. Since the precise position of the point of the attacking weapon will not be apparent to the audience, such thrusts cannot be justified on the grounds of dramatic effectiveness. Full lunges at the body which are intended to hit the target, should be delivered without the weight of the attacker behind them. The most substantial button on a reproduction weapon will not prevent the penetration of a full-blooded lunge.

In the hands of competent fencers, the small sword can be wielded at high speed. To an experienced observer who is trained to follow the moves, this can be most exciting. To a general audience, however, individual moves will not be clear and in consequence the sole justification for the fight in the theatre—its *dramatic significance*—will be nullified. In any case, two men fighting for their lives, are likely to be cautious. They will keep their moves simple. They will not engage in complex, high speed play that is likely to leave them open to a thrust through the body. General advances and retirements of the whole body, and well pointed specific movements of hands and arms, will help to show an audience the general pattern of attack and defence when the movements of the actual weapons might not be visible to it.

The style of fighting in this period is of particular importance. An actor must convince an audience that he has indeed had considerable experience in handling the weapon he is using. He must show, if he is playing the character of an eighteenth-century gentleman, that he has had that gentleman's education in the art of fence. A training in modern foil play would be a sound background for an actor, from which to study the style of small sword play.

A Plot for a 'Beaux Stratagem' Fight

The fight, from Act V, takes place between *Hounslow* and *Bagshot* on the one side, and *Aimwell* and *Archer* on the other. The scene is a room in *Lady*

Bountiful's house. All four combatants are armed with small swords. There are really two fights here that will require individual plotting; that which *Aimwell* fights, at first with both the rogues and later only with *Bagshot*, and that which *Archer* fights with *Hounslow*. Let us consider that fought by *Aimwell*.

SCRIPT	PHASE	AIMWELL	BAGSHOT	HOUNSLOW
Enter Hounslow *dragging in* Lady Bountiful, *and* Bagshot *hauling in* Dorinda;				
the Rogues with Swords drawn.				
Houn Come, come, your Jewels, Mistress.				
Bag Your Keys, your Keys, old Gentlewoman.				
Enter Aimwell *and* Cherry.				
Aim Turn this way, Villains; I durst engage an Army in such a Cause. (*He engages 'em both.*)		Draws and comes on guard		

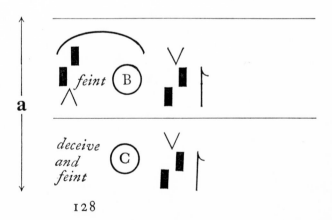

SCRIPT	PHASE	AIMWELL	BAGSHOT	HOUNSLOW

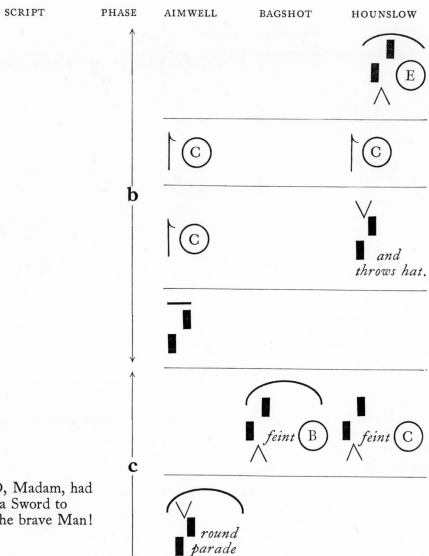

Dor O, Madam, had I but a Sword to help the brave Man!

L. Boun There's three or four hanging up in the Hall; but they won't draw. I'll go fetch one however. (*Exit.*)

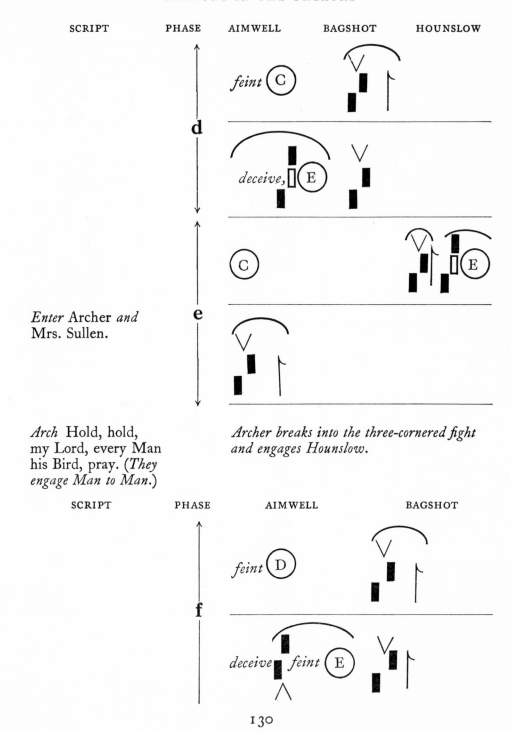

Enter Archer *and*
Mrs. Sullen.

Arch Hold, hold,
my Lord, every Man
his Bird, pray. (*They
engage Man to Man.*)

*Archer breaks into the three-cornered fight
and engages Hounslow.*

SCRIPT	PHASE	AIMWELL	BAGSHOT

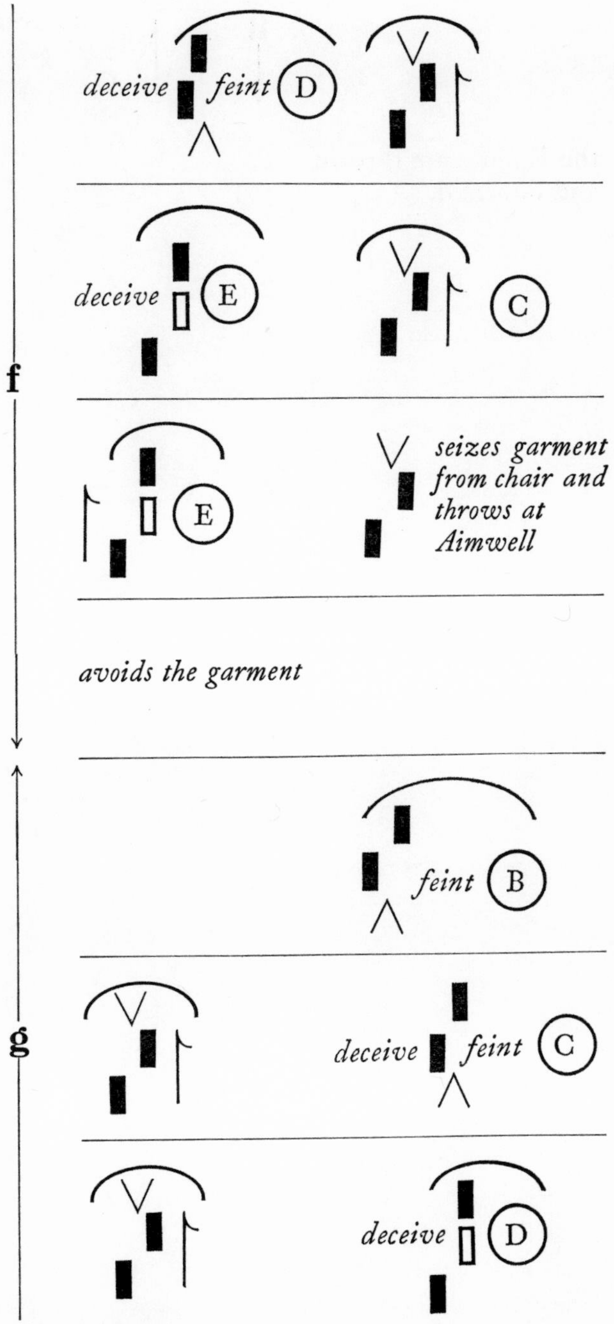

deceive *feint* (D)

deceive (E) (C)

(E) *seizes garment from chair and throws at Aimwell*

avoids the garment

feint (B)

deceive *feint* (C)

deceive (D)

f

g

SCRIPT	PHASE	AIMWELL	BAGSHOT
	$\mathbf{g}$ ↓	*and threatens with point on C*	*drops sword and capitulates*

the Rogues are thrown
and disarm'd.

Epilogue

Towards the end of the eighteenth century, the pistol had largely replaced the sword as the weapon of serious personal combat. Duels with the sword have certainly been fought as late as 1966, but they cannot be regarded as really serious affairs. The duel fought between the Marquis de Cuevas and Serge Lifar on 30 March 1958, was discontinued after a scratch had been inflicted on Lifar's forearm, and the doctors in attendance ruled that he had been put in 'a position of inferiority'.

But the *theatrical* tradition of violence continues as strongly as ever. The code of the British Independent Television Authority has a good deal to say about violence, indicating that as an aspect of drama it is still very much with us. *Journey's End* is set entirely in an atmosphere of terrifying physical violence; so is *The Long and the Short and the Tall*. Such popular British television series as *The Avengers*, *Z Cars*, *No Hiding Place* and *Danger Man*, all have physical violence as a recurrent major theme, though the weapons now might range from the hand grenade and the laser beam to the broken bottle and the bicycle chain. American television is by no means immune. Violence is central to such series as *Law Man*, *Gun Law* and *The Untouchables*. In film, violence is international. It is an essential element of the *Bond* films. *The Bridge on the River Kwai* and *A Town Like Alice* are set in violence and contain many violent incidents that are essential to the dramatic achievement. *Rashomon* is a study in violence. Outside what we might regard as the legitimate media of dramatic entertainment, the dramatic element of violence exists as a central theme. No one who has been present at a modern wrestling bout, can deny the dramatic element in the display. Moves seem timed deliberately to provoke a particular audience response. The audience participates vigorously; it is amused, entertained, horrified and occasionally moved. It has its heroes and its villains, which are not the wrestlers themselves so much as the characters they create. In the widest sense, the experience is cathartic.

Violence is a fact of life. To ignore it, in the hope that it will go away, is ridiculous. To legislate against it, in the belief that it can be ultimately suppressed, is no less ridiculous. It is a fact that society, both national and international, must come to terms with. Drama is one medium through which this can be done.

Bibliography

ALLANSON-WINN, R. G., and PHILLIPPS-WOLLEY, C. *Broadsword and Singlestick*, The All-England Series. George Bell, London, 1890.

AYLWARD, J. D. *The Small Sword in England*. Hutchinson, London, 1945.

AYLWARD, J. D. *The House of Angelo*. Batchworth Press, London, 1953.

AYLWARD, J. D. *The English Master of Arms*. Routledge and Kegan Paul, London, 1956.

BALDICK, ROBERT *The Duel*. Chapman and Hall, London, 1965.

BLACKMORE, HOWARD L. *Arms and Armour*. Studio Vista, London, 1965.

BROOKS, F. W. *The Battle of Stamford Bridge*. East Yorkshire Historical Society, York, 1956.

BURKE, EDMUND *The History of Archery*. Heinemann, London, 1958.

CARY, M. and others (eds.) *The Oxford Classical Dictionary*. The Clarendon Press, Oxford, 1949.

CASTLE, EGERTON *Schools and Masters of Fence*. George Bell, London, 1885.

CROSNIER, ROGER *Fencing with the Foil*. Faber and Faber, London, 1951.

CROSNIER, ROGER *Fencing with the Sabre*. Faber and Faber, London, 1954.

CROSNIER, ROGER *Fencing with the Épée*. Faber and Faber, London, 1958.

ELLEHAUGE, MARTIN *The Spear*. N. Olaf Møller, Copenhagen, 1948.

FFOULKES, CHARLES J. *The Armouries of the Tower of London*. Vols. I and II. Her Majesty's Stationery Office, London, 1916.

FFOULKES, CHARLES J., and HOPKINSON, CAPTAIN E. C. *Sword, Lance and Bayonet*. Cambridge, London, 1938.

FORESTIER, AMÉDÉE *The Roman Soldier*. A. & C. Black, London, 1928.

GIORGETTI, G. *Armi Bianche*. Associazione Amatori Armi Antiche, Milan, 1961.

HAYWARD, J. F. *Armour*. Her Majesty's Stationery Office, London, 1951.

HAYWARD, J. F. *Swords and Daggers*. Her Majesty's Stationery Office, London, 1951.

HUTTON, CAPTAIN ALFRED *Cold Steel*. Clowes, London, 1889.

LABAN, RUDOLF *Principles of Dance and Movement Notation*. Macdonald and Evans, London, 1956.

MANN, SIR WILLIAM Wallace Collection Catalogues, *European Arms and Armour*. Vols. I and II. Wallace Collection, London, 1962.

OAKESHOTT, R. EWART *The Archeology of Weapons*. Lutterworth, London, 1960.

OAKESHOTT, R. EWART *A Knight and his Armour*. Lutterworth, London, 1961.

OAKESHOTT, R. EWART *The Sword in the Age of Chivalry*. Lutterworth, London, 1964.

ONIONS, C. T. and others (eds.) *Shakespeare's England*, Vols. I and II. Clarendon Press, Oxford, 1917.

POLLOCK, W. H., GROVE, F. C., MITCHELL, E. B., and ARMSTRONG, W. *Fencing, Boxing, Wrestling*. The Badminton Library. Longmans, Green, London, 1890.

SANDYS, SIR JOHN EDWIN (ed.) *A Companion to Latin Studies*. Cambridge University Press, Cambridge, 3rd. ed. 1943.

SILVER, G. *Paradoxes of Defence*. Shakespeare Association Facsimiles No. 6. Oxford University Press, London, 1933.

SJØVOLD, THORLEIF *The Oseberg Find*. Universitetes Oldsaksamling, Oslo, 1957.

SMITH, WILLIAM and others (eds.) *A Dictionary of Greek and Roman Antiquities*. Vols. I and II. John Murray, London, 3rd. ed. 1890.

SPRAGUE, A. C. *Shakespeare and the Actors*. Harvard University Press, Harvard, 3rd. imp. 1945.

TREECE, HENRY and OAKESHOTT, EWART *Fighting Men*. Brockhampton Press, Leicester, 1963.

WALKER, DONALD *Defensive Exercises*. Hurst, London, 1840.

WEBSTER, GRAHAM *The Roman Army*. Grosvenor Museum, Chester, 1956.

WEDGEWOOD, C. V. *Civil War Battlefields*. BBC Publications, London.

WHIBLEY, LEONARD (ed.) *A Companion to Greek Studies*. Cambridge University Press, Cambridge, 3rd. ed. 1916.

WICKHAM, GLYNNE *Early English Stages 1300–1600*. Vols. I and II part I. Routledge and Kegan Paul, London, 1959 and 1963.

WILKINSON, FREDERICK *Swords and Daggers*. Ward, Lock, London, 1967.

WILKINSON, HENRY *Engines of War*. Longman, Orme, Brown, Green and Longmans, London, 1841.

Antiquities of Roman Britain. The Trustees of the British Museum, London, 1947.

'On Fencing with the Two Handed Sword' in *Reliquiae Antiquae*. Vol. I. Pickering, 1841. (A copy exists in the library of the University of Nottingham.)

'Rapier and Dagger' in *A New Book of Sports*, reprinted from the *Saturday Review*. Richard Bentley and Son, London, 1885.

The Sutton Hoo Ship Burial. The Trustees of the British Museum, London, 1947.

War and the Chase. A handbook to the collection of weapons of savage, barbaric, and civilized peoples, in the Horniman Museum. London County Council, London, 1929.

Index

FORM 109